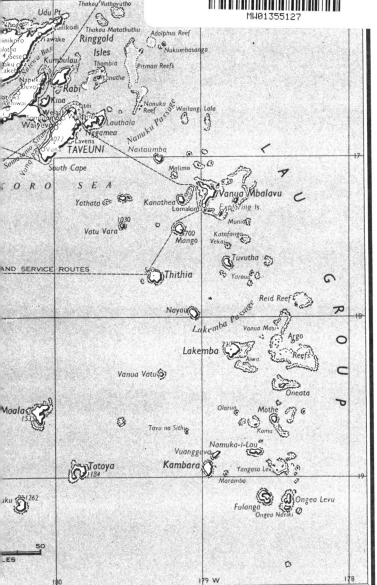

MYTHS & LEGENDS
of
Fiji
& Rotuma

MYTHS & LEGENDS
of
Fiji
& Rotuma

A.W. REED AND INEZ HAMES

Illustrated by ROGER HART

REED

Published by Reed Books, a division of Reed Publishing (NZ)
Ltd, 39 Rawene Road, Birkenhead, Auckland. Associated
companies, branches and representatives throughout the world.

This book is copyright. Except for the purpose of fair reviewing,
no part of this publication may be reproduced or transmitted in
any form or by any means, electronic or mechanical, including
photocopying, recording, or any information storage and retrieval
system, without permission in writing from the publisher.
Infringers of copyright render themselves liable to prosecution.

ISBN 0 7900 0298 1

© 1967 Literary Productions Ltd

First published 1967
Reprinted 1993, 1994

Cover design by Claire Preen
Printed in Singapore

CONTENTS

CHAPTER I LEGENDS OF DEGEI AND THE SPIRIT WORLD	*page*
The Creation of Men and Women	13
The Great Flood	16
The Sons of Degei	18
The Hazardous Road to Bulu	21
The Great Serpent of Nakauvadra	26
The Terrible Son of the Sky King	29
CHAPTER II LEGENDS OF THE GODS	
The Great Drum of Matakano	37
The Man Who Was Used as a Ball	39
The Rolling Head of the God	47
The Lady of the Sky	48
Gods Who Fought for their Women	51
The God of the Summit of Gau	58
The God Who Turned Himself into a Rat	62
CHAPTER III RATU-MAI-BULU THE SNAKE GOD	
How the Island of Viwa was Built	69
The Chief Who Challenged a God	73
The Battle of the Ghost and the God	76
CHAPTER IV DAKUWAQA THE SHARK GOD	
The Battle of Shark and Octopus	83
The Land that Went to Sea	86
The Shark God	90
The Shark Who Swam Away from Home	92
CHAPTER V ISLAND VOYAGES AND DISCOVERIES	
How the Men of Livuka Came to Lakeba	97
Why Ono is Far Away from Lakeba	104
Food and Water from Moala	107
How the Island of Rotuma was Made	109
How Bua Got its Name	112
How Yanuca Got its Name	114

CHAPTER VI THE MAKING OF ISLANDS

	page
Why Moce is larger than Oneata	119
How the Sandhills of Nadroga were Made	121
Molau and Tanova	122

CHAPTER VII LEGENDS OF GIANTS

Flaming Teeth	127
A Giant and his Swing	129
The Giant Who Went to Look for Water	131
Kumaku and the Giant	133
Ravouvou the Dart Thrower	135
Suna Who was Greedy	137

CHAPTER VIII MONSTERS AND SUPERNATURAL CREATURES

The Monster of Cakaudrove	143
The Phantom Canoe	147
The Skirt of Intestines	149
The Friendly Gnomes of the Forest	151

CHAPTER IX LEGENDS OF SNAKES

The Snake Chief	155
The Gigantic Snake	158

CHAPTER X LEGENDS OF FISH

The Prawns of Vatulele	163
The Boundary Quarrel	166
No Shellfish or Parrots in Bureta	169
The Fish of the Swamp	170

CHAPTER XI LEGENDS OF BIRDS AND INSECTS

How the Crabs Deceived the Heron	175
The Crane and the Butterfly	177
Why the Rooster Crows when the Tide is Rising	178
How Mosquitoes Came to Oneata	181

CHAPTER XII LEGENDS OF ANIMALS

How Dau-lawaki Ate the Sacred Cat	187
The Rat and the Flying Fox	191
Why Pigs Dig for Worms	194

CONTENTS

CHAPTER XIII LEGENDS OF FLOWERS AND FRUIT

page

How Serua Got its Name	199
The Tagimoucia Flowers	200
The Lost Orange	202
How Bananas Came to Fiji	204
The Vanishing Breadfruit	206

CHAPTER XIV LEGENDS OF TREES AND PLANTS

The Gods Who Exchanged Trees	209
The Turtle Nuts of the Vonu Tree	211
How the Moon was Trapped	214
How Sugar Cane Came to Rotuma	217
How the Via Plant was Taken to Rewa	220
The Vine that Stooped Over Tonga	222
The First Vadra Tree	225

CHAPTER XV FOLK TALES

The Boy Whose Name Was One-Hair	229
The Woman Who Emptied the Sea	232
The Boy Who Was Hungry	233
The Etiquette of Eating	234
A Petrified Feast	235
The Fire Walkers of Beqa	236

CHAPTER XVI TALES OF ROMANCE

The Dart Throwing Competition	239
The Turtle of the Sky King	242
The Flood that Carried a Feast	248
Three Presents for the Chief's Daughter	250

ILLUSTRATIONS

The boy went up to strike him with his fist	*page* 31
The young man was tossed from one to another	41
They rushed together and the sound of falling weapons crashed like thunder	78
To his surprise he found himself brought up with a jerk	84
She heard the beating of wings and looked up to see a huge bird flying overhead	99
He saw his friend running with the baskets on his shoulder	123
The party was over; all the food was eaten	138
She was absorbed in her task	144
Out of its body came Ramatau and Rivaele, alive and well	159
Buisavalu walked up to Lovoni with the sea at her heels	167
He inadvertently placed his foot in the shell of a clam	179
"Is *that* your god?"	189
She kept on running not knowing where she was going	201
"Foolish mortal. Why are you hiding there?"	212
The unsuspecting Aiatos was caught in the net and pulled upwards	218
He pressed his hands over his eyes and took no notice of fish, wind, or birds	243

PREFACE

The colony of Fiji consists of two main islands, Viti Levu and Vanua Levu, and a number of smaller ones, including Taveuni, Kadavu, Rabi, Vatulele, Beqa, and Qamea. In addition there are several important groups of islands – Lomaiviti, Lau, and Yasawa. Altogether there are over 300 islands. Rotuma to the north, is administered by Fiji but is not part of the colony proper.

The legends related in this book come from all parts of Fiji, and as many place names appear in the stories, a study of the map on the end papers will prove rewarding. Viti Levu, with Suva on the southern coast, has an area of 4,000 square miles, Vanua Levu over 2,000 square miles, and the adjacent island of Taveuni an area of 168 square miles.

The principal groups are:

Lau Islands, to the east, consisting of fifty-seven islands.

Moala Islands, to the south-east; three islands which are part of the Lau group.

Lomaiviti, in the Koro Sea, immediately to the east of Viti Levu, twelve islands.

Kadavu, south of Viti Levu, consisting of the main islands, Kadavu and Ono, and a number of smaller ones.

Yasawa, a chain of twenty islands running north west of Viti Levu.

Rotuma, 400 miles north of Suva, is only eight miles long and two miles wide. It is the largest of a small group of eight islands.

Fijians are predominantly Melanesian throughout most of the groups, but these are widely scattered over nearly 10,000 square miles of ocean, and the boldness of early sea rovers produced a mixture of racial types and cultures, Melanesian and Polynesian, even in the main islands.

Not only are the Fijians a happy and attractive race, but their legends show the best traits of both Melanesia and Polynesia. There is imagination, love of nature in all its aspects as well as some fear, and happiness and laughter that pervade many of the folk tales. Tongan and Samoan influences can be traced in some of the legends.

Although there are now more Indians than Fijians in the colony, together with a smaller number of Europeans and Chinese, the Fijians are the indigenous people, and the legends retold here are of Fijian origin, together with a few tales from far-distant Rotuma, whose people are of almost pure Polynesian ancestry.

A number of books have been consulted for the present compilation, amongst them *Tales from Old Fiji*, Lorimer Fison; *The Lau Islands*, T. R. St Johnston; *Fiji and the Fijians*, Thomas Williams; *Viti*, Berthold Seaman; *Tales from the South Seas*, Anne Gittings; and the articles of Mrs Richenda Parham in the *Fiji Times*. Grateful acknowledgment is made to C. R. H. Taylor, compiler of the *Pacific Bibliography*, for personal help and for the assistance afforded by his indispensable book.

Although all the legends have been retold by A. W. Reed, and the different versions compared and reconciled for the sake of consistency, the book could not have been compiled without the material collected so diligently by Miss Inez Hames. *Legends of Fiji and Rotuma* was published privately by Miss Hames in 1960 and is now out of print. Miss Hames has generously made this material available and has gathered other stories, not previously published, to enrich the collection. She expresses gratitude to Miss Ruth Pook in gathering stories from the girls of the Ballantine Memorial School, and to Mrs Alena Cavu, Ratu Isikeli Daveta, and the late Miss Daisy Lucas and Peceli Neisua.

Readers who are unfamiliar with the Fijian language, or with Fijian place names, should note that some sounds are not represented by the conventional letters with which Europeans are familiar.

c is pronounced th
b is pronounced mb
d is pronounced nd
g is pronounced ng
q is pronounced ng-g

The following names are given as written and as pronounced: Degei (Ndengei); Cibaciba (Thimbathimba); Yaqona (Yang-gona).

On the endpaper map examples of both systems of nomenclature will be found.

A. W. REED

CHAPTER I
LEGENDS OF DEGEI AND THE SPIRIT WORLD

THE CREATION OF MEN AND WOMEN

IN the beginning of time, the great, the ever-living god, the Great Serpent Degei lived alone without friends or companions. The only living creature he saw was Turukawa, the hawk, that flew round his home. Although it could not speak, the little hawk became the constant friend of the mighty god.

Degei came out of his house one morning and listened for the accustomed whirr of wings, but there was no sound but the soft stirring of leaves, the sigh of the wind, and the chatter of a nearby stream. Then came a rustle of raindrops which turned to a steady downpour. The god looked everywhere, but still there was no sign of his friend. Sadly he turned and went inside his house.

Every morning he looked out expectantly, but every morning he was disappointed. The loneliness oppressed him, and he longed more and more for the company of his little friend. It was on a day when the sun was shining and the song of the stream was ringing in his ears that he heard the flutter of wings. He ran outside and saw the hawk settling in the long grass.

"Welcome! Welcome!" he cried. "I have missed you. The days have been so long without you."

He knew that the hawk could not speak, but he was surprised and disappointed when she took no notice of him. She flew away and came back with a tuft of grass in her beak. Many times the hawk flew away and returned again. Degei was puzzled and wondered what she could be doing with the leaves and soft grass that she brought. He walked over and looked down. The long grass was flattened down and in the middle of the clear space was a nest of soft grass and downy feathers.

"What are you doing, little bird?" asked the Great Serpent with a smile. The hawk flitted between his legs and was gone again.

It was a puzzled god who returned to his house. He felt that his friend had deserted him.

The next day he went back to the nest. Two eggs lay there. Then he realised what had happened. He knew that he could never win back the hawk's affection, for she had found a mate and soon would have two fledglings to occupy her time.

He struck his forehead with his fist. "What is the use of being a god if I don't use my power?" he murmured.

He scooped the eggs up in his hand and carried them tenderly to his house, where he made a soft bed for them and warmed them with his own body. Weeks and months went by and the eggs lay warm against his side. He began to wonder whether they would ever hatch, but at last his patience was rewarded. The shells broke, and two tiny human babies gave a thin cry. They were his children as truly as those of Turukawa.

Tenderly he lifted them up and carried them to a vesi tree. He built a shelter for them, and fed them on scraps of food. They grew quickly, but they did not move from their tree. They were the first children in the world and they had no one to teach them except the Great Serpent, who was so great a god that he did not understand the needs of growing children. All he could do was to talk to them and tell them the secrets of nature. When they cried he brought more food, and marvelled at their appetites. To save himself work he planted banana trees, yams, and dalo close to them. When the bananas formed on the trees they ate them and sang with delight; but the yams and dalo they could not eat because Degei had not thought to teach them the art of firemaking, and they could not eat them raw.

All the time the children were unaware of each other's presence, because the god had put them on opposite sides of the vesi tree. By the time they were six years old they were fully grown. One was a man, strong and broad-shouldered. The other was a woman with smooth limbs and swelling breasts and dark melting eyes.

At length the man left the shelter where he had grown up from babyhood to boyhood and then to manhood in so short a time, and gazed down with admiration at the woman, who looked up at him with a soft light in her eyes.

"Come to me," said the man, holding out his arms. "Degei has made us for each other. Our children will people the whole earth."

With his arm round her shoulders he went to Degei and said, "We are tired of eating bananas."

"They are the best food, my son."

"Maybe; but one gets tired of eating the best food all the time."

"There are yams and dalo. You never touch them, but they also are the food of the gods."

"They taste so bad and are so hard that we cannot eat them."

"Have you ever cooked them?"

"Cook? We don't know how to cook. You have never told us how it is done."

"Come with me, then," Degei said. "I will show you."

He dug a hole in the ground, showed the children of his creation how to kindle fire and heat stones, and how to cook root vegetables in the earth oven. They were quick to learn. The Great Serpent watched them proudly and thought how pleasant it was to have two companions to talk to.

After a little while they left him, as the hawk had done years before, but Degei knew they would come back.

When they returned the woman carried a newborn baby in her arms and the man looked as though he would even defy a god if harm threatened his son. Degei knew then that gods cannot mate with human beings, and that like to like is a law of human beings as well as of birds.

He was not unhappy as he went back to his house and saw them strolling down the valley, for he knew that from his loneliness had come men and women who would people the world and worship him as their god.

THE GREAT FLOOD

Turukawa, the favourite hawk that belonged to the god Degei, had been killed by the two sons of the god. As it fell it made scars on the face of the cliff, and dyed the leaves of the vau trees with its blood. Degei had the boys brought before him and reproved them severely. The boys were insolent.

"We have done nothing wrong," one of them growled. "It was only a hawk, which is not even good for food."

"But Turukawa was my friend," Degei said sadly.

Both boys broke into mocking laughter.

"You must be hard up for friends," they shouted insolently as they slouched back to their own village.

"Come and help us," they called to their friends. "Degei has treated us like children, but we are grown men and we won't be spoken to as if we were young boys."

"You will certainly need help if you have insulted Degei," an old man said sourly. "He is slow to anger and good to those who respect him, but in punishment he is terrible to behold."

There was jeering laughter from the young men and their friends.

"We don't care," they shouted. "We are strong. We'll build a big wall round our village and old Degei can do his worst."

For three months they worked hard, felling trees, lopping off the branches, and planting them deep in the ground. They lashed poles between the palisades and strong saplings close together. During this time Degei gathered an army together and besieged the village. His warriors tried to cut the lashings, but as soon as they approached the stockade, spears and stones flew from the defences and drove them back. Using all the arts of warfare, the attackers strove to break down the stockade, but every time they were driven back.

Degei saw that there was little chance of his men breaching the defences. He dismissed them, and returned to his house, determined to visit a terrible fate on his rebellious descendants. Standing in the doorway looking down the long valley, he spoke words of power; dark clouds rolled up from the sea until the gloom of evening enveloped the land. At another word from the god the clouds poured down their floods of water. Every stream became a raging torrent, waterfalls sprang from the steep hillsides, avalanches of mud and stones spread over the valley, blocking the lower reaches, and muddy water welled slowly up the long slope. Soon it was lapping at the palisades, pouring between the saplings, engulfing the buildings, mounting steadily, inexorably upwards.

At first the villagers had been amused, thinking the display of power would soon expend itself, but sheets of rain continued to drive down like spears; one by one they were overcome and borne away. The two young men were perched on the roof of the house. Their laughter was spent, and now in terror they cried to the god to save them.

"We are sorry for our evil ways. Send back these waters and we shall do whatever you want," they cried.

For the first time for months Degei addressed them.

"It is a great evil you have done to your people as well as to me. The water cannot be turned back to its source. It will rise now until even the mountain tops are covered."

"What shall we do?" wept the boys. "There are only six people left of all who lived here, and soon we shall all be drowned."

"Are you truly sorry?" Degei demanded.

"Yes, yes," they all cried.

The god stooped down and launched the fruit of a shaddock on the waters. It floated towards them.

"Get in quickly," he commanded, and the eight survivors of the flood scrambled on to the shaddock fruit. It was borne away on the water and floated high over the flooded trees. Soon there was nothing to be seen but a waste of swirling waters.

"The world has come to an end," the bewildered survivors muttered; but presently the rain stopped, the sun came out, and the water began to subside. The fruit grounded on the mountain top of Beqa and they stepped out on to the sodden ground and watched the flood ebbing slowly down the valleys.

A new world had begun. Two tribes had disappeared completely – one a tribe of women, the other of men and women who had tails like animals. They were never seen again.

And on the highest point of the island of Koro, on the peak called Qiqi-tagici-koro, stood a little qiqi bird which sang a mournful song:

"The qiqi laments over Koro, because it is lost."

THE SONS OF DEGEI

GREATEST of all Fijian gods was Degei the Snake God, creator of Viti Levu and Vanua Levu and all the smaller islands. At first the world was in a state of chaos. Degei sent one of his sons, Rokomoutu, to arrange the land in an orderly fashion. Where Rokomoutu's garment dragged across the land, sandy beaches appeared; when he tucked it up, the shore became rocky or covered with mangrove bushes.

The other sons of Degei were Rokola, the eldest, who was a carpenter; Uto; and Nagai the messenger.

The house of Degei-the-all-powerful was in a cave in the mountain range Nakauvadra. The mouth of the cave was guarded by a curtain of snakes which hung head downwards.

When Degei turned over in his sleep, people said: "It is thunder!"

One night the god was awakened by the noise of the surf on the reef of the Raki-raki coast, and he peevishly ordered one of his sons to go to stop the noise so that he could sleep. Now the surf still breaks on the reef, but it does so quietly, because of its fear of the great god.

Sensitive to noise, Degei was awakened again by men beating clay into shape as they made pots and bowls. With his foot Degei pushed the land where the potters were working and broke it off, thrusting it into the sea, potters and all, where it became two islands.

Bats, too, aggravated the god. Nagai the messenger was sent to drive away the flying foxes, who make a noise with their shrill cries and the clapping of their leathery wings. Nagai cut down a large nokonoko tree, lopped off the branches, and threw the home-made club at the bats. They scattered before it and the club flew on and fell into the sea past the point of Naicobocobo. Nagai waded out, picked it up, put it over his shoulder, and came ashore.

Unseen eyes were watching him from the shelter of the trees. It was a Vuya god, who could hardly believe that anyone could carry a whole tree so lightly and so carelessly. He ran to tell his friends, who were also gods. They went to see for themselves, and were so impressed by Nagai's strength that they gave him a great feast, and when he left they begged him to visit them again.

LEGENDS OF DEGEI AND THE SPIRIT WORLD 19

Nagai took a liking to these gods and some time later went back to Naicobocobo to visit them. In honour of his coming they prepared the biggest feast that had ever been made. The cooked food was piled in rows higher than a man and hundreds of feet in length. Nagai sat down and began to eat, steadily devouring row after row of food and leaving none for the others. For a while they sat speechless in admiration of his prowess, which was as great as his strength; but when they realised that there would be nothing left for them, their admiration turned to anger.

"Let us kill this greedy fellow before he devastates the whole district," they said. They tried to entice him into one of their houses when all the food was finished, but Nagai could read their minds.

"I never sleep in another house," he said.

"But you have no house of your own here."

"I will have soon," replied the god. He went to the forest, uprooted a number of trees, stripped off the branches, and drove the posts into the ground. Deftly he covered them with heavy branches and laced the smaller ones and foliage into the roof, thatching it securely against the rain.

"This is my house," he said. "Let no one enter," and went inside.

"Greedy though he may be, we would do well not to offend him," they thought. "If we bring gifts he would no doubt leave us alone and regard us as his friends."

So they went to their own houses and fetched gifts to lay in front of Nagai's doorway – fishing nets, pots, hooks, sandwood, fruit, mats, and carved paddles.

"It is well," Nagai grunted. "Now I will make my gift to you. Build me a strong wall to enclose an open space."

They made a fence of stakes driven into the ground, interlaced with sticks and branches.

"Make it bigger; *much* bigger."

When it was finished he opened his arm band, took out a hundred pigs, and placed them in the pen. From his ear he took a piece of masi cloth which he wore as an ornament, and pulled it out. It seemed never to come to an end. Fold after fold lay on the ground and was piled up high above the level of the roof of the house.

"It is all for you," Nagai said shortly, and retired into his house. That night there was great rejoicing. Further provisions were brought from a distance and the yaqona bowl passed round and round the circle of gods.

But Nagai did not join them. He brooded in his house, remembering they had planned treachery against him. He left in the early morning, and when the gods woke up they found that their own chief was dead.

In Raki-raki the spirit of fear has never left the village. It broods over the clearing and the past like an evil spirit, and the people of Vuya take care never to be in Raki-raki at night.

THE HAZARDOUS ROAD TO BULU

THE jumping off place for the spirits of the dead was the sacred headland at Naicobocobo, which was guarded by Lewalevu, the goddess who tries to intercept souls passing on their way to Bulu. She was usually circumvented by making offerings of leaves.

The second of many tests and ordeals was provided by the famous sandalwood tree at Vuniyasikinikini. Whether a man had been industrious or idle in his life was soon proved, for his spirit was required to pinch the trunk of the yasi tree with his fingernails. If they penetrated the bark he was judged to be lazy, his fingernails having grown long with disuse; but if they were too short, then it was known that he had been an industrious and hard-working man.

While problems may continually beset married men, to be unmarried is even worse, for there are few, if any, unfortunate bachelors who manage to reach the place of everlasting life in the spirit world of Bulu. When the bachelor dies his soul must first evade the clutches of Lewalevu. The soul of the unmarried man has little difficulty in escaping her. His greatest problem is to avoid Naqanaqa, the devourer of bachelors, who sits on a black stone by the edge of the sea. At high tide the water laps against the stone on one side, and on the other dank rocks tower high into the air. The only path is below Naqanaqa's seat and none can hope to pass her by unseen.

The shivering spirit of the unwed man waits until the tide is low and he can traverse the reef, hoping that when he comes to the end some fisherman will take pity on him and offer his canoe to bring him to land further along the coast. It is an empty hope. The bachelor spirit waits in vain as the tide rises and huge waves begin to thunder on the reef. To be drawn into the caverns or hurled against the sharp coral would be a second death, so the spirit dives into the calm water of the lagoon and drifts ashore. No matter how quickly he runs, Naqanaqa races towards him, lifts him up in her huge hands and dashes him against the black stone as one breaks up rotten timber for firewood.

It is easier for the spirit of a married man to reach Drakulu and Cibaciba, the portals of Bulu; but the way is still beset with difficulties. The spirit walks along a well-defined road until he comes to a solitary hill of red clay dotted with black boulders. He recognises it because of a handsome grove of trees nearby. Gladly would he rest there, but he knows he must toil up the steep slopes of the hill called Takiveleyama until he reaches the summit. Before doing so he must throw to the spirit the whale's tooth which was placed in his dead hand at a ghostly pandanus tree. If he misses his throw he will have to remain there, unhappy and alone, for it is a sign that his wife is not following him. The lonely spirit sighs and sings a mournful song:

> For long years I planted food for my wife,
> She ate it and shared it with her friends.
> They praised me as the great provider of food:
> How is it that they will not let her follow me now?
> So little is their love for me after many years of toil!
> Will no one strangle my wife
> That her spirit will be released
> To follow me to this place?

If he is fortunate, his heart will be lightened when he sees his wife, set free from her earthly body, coming towards him. Then he will bound joyfully up the hill, as one of those assured of the faithfulness of their wives; but if she does not come, his feet will drag slowly and wearily to the summit. Here there is rejoicing for those who go on accompanied by loved ones, and sorrow for all who are lonely.

The spirits now descend the hill and sooner or later come to the sea shore where the canoe waits to take them to the presence of the gods, who will examine their past lives and decide what their fate will be. Their coming is announced by a parakeet, which cries once for each ghostly occupant of the canoe of death. It is a warning to the people of Nabaqatai to set their doors open wide so that the passage of the spirits may not be impeded.

There are two villages called Nabaqatai. One is real, occupied by living people. The other Nabaqatai is of the spirit world, unreal and ghostly, and set in the same place as the living village. So it is that the men, women, and children of Nabaqatai cannot see the ghostly travellers who pass through their midst; but when the parakeet shouts his warning they speak in whispers and set their doors open wide. Every house has two doors, placed exactly opposite each other. The spirits pass through silently and leave no mark on the earthen floor.

Who can tell whether Samulayo, the Killer of Souls, belongs to the material village or the spiritual one? It may be that he lives in both simultaneously, being both a man and a spirit. While he is sitting in his house he hides among the insubstantial mangroves of the spirit world, and places a reed across the path as a sign that the spirit may go no further. A valiant soul will raise his club. Then Samulayo comes out to do battle with him, asking his name and village. If a false answer is given, Samulayo tries to kill him, and if he succeeds his ethereal body is cooked and eaten in a Nabaqatai that can belong only to the nonmaterial world. If he is wounded he wanders disconsolately through the bare mountains, seeking and never finding a permanent home. Those who defeat Samulayo in battle, or who are allowed to pass unmolested, go on to their final judgment by the great god Degei on the high peak of Naidelide in the Kauvadra mountains. The path ends abruptly at a high precipice which plunges down to a deep lake. It is a grim, mysterious place, this final judgment-seat for the souls of men; and stranger still is the enormous steering paddle that is balanced on the edge of the precipice.

In a voice that rolls and echoes round the mountains, Degei asks the fateful question: "In what manner do you come to us? What has your behaviour been in the world of living men?"

If the spirit can say truthfully, "I am a great chief. I lived as a chief and I behaved as a chief. I have destroyed many villages and killed many warriors." Degei replies "Good! Sit down on the broadest part of the paddle and let the cool breeze play on you."

As soon as the spirit is seated the god swings down on the paddle. The ghost flies high into the air and falls into the lake. With the blood booming in his ears he sinks deep into the water until he reaches Murimuria, and is taken to the district where he will find the reward that is in store for men who have pleased the gods. The same fate awaits lesser men, and none can choose for himself, for judgment is in the hands of the gods. Very occasionally they select a man of outstanding life and restore his spirit to his home, where he is deified.

Murimuria is but the outer domain of Bulu, the afterworld, where punishment is meted out to those who have offended the gods. They are placed face downwards in rows and changed into dalo plants. Those who have not troubled to have their ears bored are condemned to carry logs of wood, on which cloth is beaten, for ever on their shoulders, and to be derided by others. Women whose faces are smooth because they have not been tattooed are chased by others, who slash them with sharp shells until they are disfigured. Others are cut up and made into bread for the gods. The worst fate is reserved for warriors who have not been skilful in battle or who have not killed anyone. They are forced to beat a heap of filth with their unblooded weapons – the most degrading task that has ever been devised.

The fortunate ones go to Burotu, the land of eternal life and light, where scented groves of trees provide resting places under cool running water, and there is food from the bowls of the gods – but there are few who reach Burotu, the blessed land that lies in Bulu.

But there were sceptics, even among the Fijians.

"We don't believe a word of all this," two young men maintained.

"What do you believe, then?" one of the priests asked disapprovingly.

"There is no life after death. Our bodies decay and only the bones are left. Can you imagine a skeleton eating, catching fish, making love?"

"There are no skeletons in Burotu, you foolish boy," the priest replied. "The spirit leaves the mortal flesh at death, and it is reclothed in a larger body which never dies."

"It is all nonsense," they said, "and we'll prove it to you."

They went away and painted themselves, covering their bodies with oil and putting on new garments, as is the way with those who are newly dead. They travelled through the forest and along the beaches until they came to Naicobocobo, the place from which the spirits take their departure on their last journey to Murimuria or Burotu.

The young men got down on their knees and cried mockingly to the god, "Please give us a canoe to take us to Bulu."

To their surprise an invisible hand placed a canoe on the sand beside them. Considerably shaken, they examined it carefully and found that it was made from the timber of the breadfruit tree. They addressed the unseen giver.

"Please, sir, we are the sons of chiefs, not slaves. We ask for a canoe of chiefs."

The canoe disappeared and another took its place. It was made of ironwood. The young men looked at each other and whispered, "It is a trick. Someone is deceiving us." They burst into peals of laughter, threw their spears at it and kicked it contemptuously.

"Take it away," they jeered, "we've been fooling you. We are living men and have no intention of dying for a long time yet."

A mighty voice came from somewhere over the sea. The trees bent before it, the echoes reverberated among the hills, and the young men held up their arms to protect their eyes from flying sand and spray. They covered their ears to block out the sound; but the unseen speaker uttered words that penetrated hands, ears, and hearts.

"O foolish young men," it said. "You are unbelievers; in mockery you called for a canoe. One you rejected, and it took one of your relatives away. You asked another, and this we gave. It too was taken, and with it another of your relatives. There is death in both your houses. If you remain you will die now, in all the folly and impiety of your youth."

The voice ceased, the echoes died away, the wind was succeeded by a calm. Laughter had drained out of the young men. With fear in their hearts they hastened back to their village. Long before they reached it they heard a sound of wailing.

Their mothers were dead.

THE GREAT SERPENT OF NAKAUVADRA

DEGEI, the Great Serpent, lived on top of the hills of Nakauvadra, in Viti Levu. In the evening the Serpent God went into a cave to sleep. As soon as he had closed his eyes, darkness rushed over the world. The opening and closing of the Great Serpent's eyes were known to men as morning and night, and when he turned over in his sleep there were earthquakes.

Near the cave was a banyan tree, and in its branches there lived a black dove, whose duty it was to wake Degei from sleep. It called softly, "Kru, kru, kru." The Great Serpent opened his eyes, and as the dark night fled from the land, he cried to the Boat Builders of Viti Levu, "Wake up. It is time to begin your work."

The tribe which Degei favoured had once lived on Bau, and the people had been poor and miserable. They had no canoes for travel between the islands, and could fish only from the reefs. The Great Serpent had taken pity on them, and had shown them how to make canoes. In this way they became strong and powerful, and learned wisdom from the god himself, because he took them to live round the sacred hills of Kauvadra on the mainland. Other men came to them, and became their servants in an attempt to gain some of their knowledge and learn to build canoes for themselves.

In time the Boat Builders became proud and arrogant, and sometimes disobeyed Degei, but he endured their disobedience because of the great love he bore them. Rokola, the chief of the tribe, and his brother Kausam-baria were the chief rebels. They had come to hate the dove that roused the Great Serpent each morning and drove them to work.

"If we were to shoot the dove," Kausam-baria said, "then we would be real chiefs, and would never have to work."

Rokola looked at his brother closely. "If we did, Degei would be angry, he would punish us."

"We could fight him. We are a strong tribe and have many warriors. The Great Serpent is a god; but there is only one of him, and we are many."

"Let us get our bows and arrows," Rokola said curtly. "Meet me under the banyan tree."

Rokola took careful aim, and with his first arrow he pierced the black dove, which fell at his feet. The brothers left the dove lying dead upon the ground and fled back to their village.

That night seemed endless. When Degei woke up he sensed that something was wrong and called to his dove, "O my lazy dove, what is the matter with you? Do you want me to wake you up?"

There was no reply. He opened his eyes and the darkness melted away. There was no sign of the dove in the banyan tree, but when he looked down, he saw it lying on the ground, pierced by Rokola's arrow.

Degei's voice pealed out like thunder. He shouted, "Evil will come to you for this deed, Rokola. I have endured many things for your sake, O Boat Builders, but now you will become less than other men. I will destroy you. I will give you to the children of Bau to do with you as they will. I will scatter you among the islands, and you shall no longer be masters, but servants and slaves."

"Take no notice," Kausam-baria whispered to Rokola. "Tell him we're not afraid of him."

Rokola was emboldened by his brother's bold words.

"We are no longer your servants, Degei," he shouted. "We are our own masters. As we destroyed your dove, so shall we destroy you."

The chief ordered his men to raise high fences round their houses and fortify them. He climbed to the highest point and called again, "Do your worst. We are ready. In days to come our descendants will say 'Our fathers ate the Great Serpent that lived on the hill of Kauvadra!'"

The god mocked them.

"Build your fences high, Rokola. Build them very high. Let them tower up to the sky, for it is a god you are defying."

Then Degei stood and threw his club up into the sky. It shattered the clouds to fragments and they fell to earth as rain. Never had such a downpour been seen. It filled the whole earth, and the sea foamed up to meet it. Waves flattened the high fences of the Boat Builders and flooded their village until nothing was seen but floating leaves and twigs, and a few canoes.

Rokola and Kausam-baria and many of their followers were killed. Only a few men and women escaped in the battered canoes. They drifted over the desolate ocean until they grounded on mountain peaks which showed above the swollen waters. They were rescued by tribes which had gathered there to escape the flood, and when it receded they were taken down to the coast to become the servants of other men.

The banyan tree had been carried away in the flood. It came to rest at Vatulele, which was nothing more than a barren reef in the middle of the sea. There was so much earth clinging to it that when it grounded it formed an island and took root, and became a refuge for men.

THE TERRIBLE SON OF THE SKY KING

AT Lakeba there lived a boy whose mother came from Tonga, and whose father was the Sky King. He was a lonely boy, and worried his mother by not joining with the other boys in their games.

"Why don't you play with the others in the rara?" she asked him. "Some day you will be sorry. They think you are too proud for them. When you become a man and are ready to go to war you will have no one to accompany you, because everyone will hate you."

"I will tell you, Mother. All the boys have fathers who talk to them and show them how to use weapons. They even play games with them. I have no father, and so I have to learn everything by myself. But I am learning fast. You will see. The day will soon come when my spear will fly to its mark more swiftly than theirs, and my club will crush their skulls."

His mother was worried by what he said.

"Listen, my son. You have a father. Truly you have a father who is greater than any other father in this village, but I do not dare to tell you who he is. If I did, you would want to go and look for him, and I should be left alone."

The boy looked at his mother coldly.

"I am nearly a man," he said quietly. "Tell me who my father is, and where I may find him."

Then his mother knew that she could not keep her son with her any longer. She wept, as mothers do.

"Tell me, Mother, or I will kill you."

She dried her eyes and said proudly, "Your father is the Sky King, the lord who is greater than any other."

The boy left her, armed himself with a stick, and disappeared into the forest. He laughed to himself, for now he knew who his father was, and that the blood of gods ran in his veins. He slashed at the flowers with his moko-moko (ironwood) stick, and as the blossoms fell he boasted to himself, "So will I treat the heads of my enemies. I am the son of the Sky King."

When night came and he was still in the forest, he set his stick upright in the ground and went to sleep. In the morning he found that it had taken root and had grown into a huge tree. The trunk soared above the other forest trees and stretched its branches up to the sky.

The boy saw that it made a ladder by which he could climb from earth to sky. He climbed up it, and came to another world, where plants and trees, and running water, and men and women were to be found.

He cried out in a loud voice, "Where are you, Sky King? I have come from Earth to Sky to find you."

The Sky King came out of the forest and looked at him closely. "Who are you?" he asked suspiciously, for he had been hiding from enemies who had driven him out of his home.

"I am your son, the Child-who-challenges-men."

"Come closer, my son, so that I can see you properly. You are such a miserable child. Why did your mother not wait until you had grown into a man before sending you to me?"

The Sky King's companions laughed at the boy. The boy smiled, but his eyes were hard and cold.

He went up to the man who was laughing loudest and struck him so hard with his fist that the man fell senseless to the ground. The laughter stopped abruptly, and the Sky King clapped his hands.

"Well done, my son," he shouted. "Perhaps you are a man after all, in spite of your size. Here, take my club and show me what you can do with the man who mocked you."

The warrior was sitting up, with a puzzled expression on his face. The boy lifted the club with both hands and struck the man such a blow that his skull was crushed, and the club was buried in his head. He threw the weapon at his father's feet and said, "Now you have seen what your son can do, it is time for me to go. I shall return to my mother, for I see that you have no need of boys to help you."

The Sky King caught the boy's hand and laughed.

"You are a firebrand, my son. You are indeed no boy, but a man among men. Stay with me and share our feast tonight, that you may be ready to come with us to assail our enemies tomorrow. You are indeed my son."

The boy employed the early hours of the evening in making a club for himself. When morning came the King's enemies approached and shouted defiance. The Child-who-challenges-men stepped forward and said, "This is my affair. No one must follow me. I will deal with these vain braggarts myself."

He rushed among the men, brandishing his club and laying

The boy went up to strike him with his fist.

about him so fiercely that many were killed and the remainder fled into the forest.

The boy called to those who remained in the village, "Come, take your dead away."

A mournful procession came out of the village, singing the death song to the accompaniment of the death-roll played on the laki (death drum). Forty-two bodies were dragged away.

Five times the Child-who-challenges-men defeated his father's enemies, until the Sky King's foes could withstand him no longer. Their souls were made small and they sent messengers to the King, asking for pardon.

So peace came to the Sky Land, and the Sky King reigned over his people again. His son sat at his side and was both honoured and feared by the people of the land.

The Child-who-challenges-men grew tall and strong, but days of peace were not to his liking, and he grew restless.

"The time has come for me to go back to Earth, which is my other home, for I wish to find a wife."

His father agreed with him, kissed him goodbye, and hastened him on his way, not through affection, but because he had come to fear his warlike son.

The young man marched to the place where he had first set foot in the Sky Land, only to find that the tree which he had climbed had been swept away by floods. Somehow he managed to get back to another island, but none know how he bridged the gap between sky and earth. We do know that he was accompanied by two white-skinned men who were gods, and that they arrived at Beqa. No one knew who he was, but it was soon apparent that a mighty warrior had appeared in their midst, for he slew all who opposed him. When he had conquered the whole land he gave half of it to the gods who had come to earth with him, and the other half to the King of Rewa.

Not satisfied with these conquests, he travelled on from island to island, overcoming all opposition, and forcing men and women to make peace offerings to him. In this way he conquered many islands, including Bau and the inland regions of Viti Levu, until at length he came to the hills of Kauvadra, where the Great Serpent lived. Degei came out to meet the son of the Sky God, saying, "Why should we fight each other, O Slayer-who-came-from-the-sky? Here is my daughter, Lady Sweet-eyes. Marry her, and we may live in peace."

So the young man married the daughter of Degei, and the two

gods leagued together. The Slayer-who-came-from-heaven continued his conquest of the islands, and eventually came to Lakeba. Ratu-mai-na-koro, the Lord-who-came-from-the-village, invited him to Tubou, and sat down with him in his house. His visitor told him how he had put the islands under subjection.

"This is good to my ears," Ratu said. "I would entertain you as a god, but alas, I have no food to offer you. The Lords of Waci-waci have oppressed us and robbed us. All I can give you is a meal of bananas. I shall pick a bunch from the tree and we shall eat together."

"Stay where you are," the Slayer-who-came-from-heaven commanded. "I will bring them to you."

He went to the tree, where he was seen by the villagers. They crowded around and said, "What are you doing by our tree? Those bananas are tabu."

"Why are they tabu?"

"We have not taken the first fruits to the lords of Waci-waci," they told him. "Until then, no one may touch them."

"I know nothing of the lords of Waci-waci," growled the Stranger-who-came-from-the-sky. He tugged at a branch of ripe bananas and put it under his arm. With a cry of rage the villagers fell on him. Still holding the bunch of fruit, the Slayer-who-came-from-the-sky smote the people with his bare fist, killing two and hurting others so that they fell to the ground. Taking no notice of the horror-stricken villagers, he strode through their ranks and put the bananas in front of the Lord-who-came-from-the-village, and said, "Let us eat."

The next day he went to other villages. His reputation had preceded him, and everywhere he was received with deep respect and presented with peace offerings. Only at Waci-waci was he repulsed, and in his anger he destroyed the men of that place.

Then he returned to Tubou, where he was received obsequiously by chiefs from many villages. The Lord-who-came-from-the-village bowed before him and said, "I am not willing to stand before you, O Slayer-who-came-from-Heaven. You must rule over my people and over all the villages."

Then the Slayer-who-came-from-Heaven ruled over the land. He sent for his wife, the Lady Sweet-eyes, the daughter of Degei. A son was born to them, and they named him Taliaitupou, from whom the lords of Nayau are descended.

The Slayer-who-came-from-Heaven then accepted the third title, the Lord of Lakeba, by which he will always be remembered.

He ruled over his people for many years, but when he grew old he gave his kingdom to his son and went to Tonga, whose people he conquered. Finally he returned to his father, the Sky King.

But in all the following generations, the descendants of Taliaitupou who ruled the kingdom called themselves the Lords of Nayau. They did not dare to accept the title of Lord of Lakeba, lest the terrible Slayer-who-came-from-Heaven should descend from the Sky Land once more and crush their skulls with a single blow of his fist.

CHAPTER II

LEGENDS OF THE GODS

THE GREAT DRUM OF MATOKANO

FIERCE wars raged across Ono until all the villages were burnt and the land itself was devastated. Eventually the men of Matokano were victorious, and their chief, Tui Matokano, became the king and warlord of Ono.

But even in Matokano it was sad to see the havoc that had been wrought. Houses were burnt to the ground, the people were hungry, and the canoes were too damaged to be put to sea.

Tui Matokano's first duty was to see that his own village was restored to its former state. The women set to work to weave mats, the men to rebuild the houses. The only material that was lacking was the fine vesi wood for the making of bowls, canoes, and other objects. It could be obtained only from the island of Kabara.

Many things were made, that the people of Matokano might trade with their friends at Kabara. After months of work the bartering took place, and the men returned with four canoes and many bowls and, most important of all, a drum of red polished vesi timber, smooth as a water-worn stone and as tall as half a man.

Tui Matokano gazed at it proudly. The old drum had been broken during the fighting; the new one was more than worthy to take its place.

When the men and women heard the rich deep voice of the drum they were enchanted with it, and forgot how close they had been to death on their way back from Kabara. Worse still, Tui Matokano forgot the vows he had made to Ligadua, the one-armed god and protector of his people.

On the homeward voyage a sudden storm had sprung up. It raged throughout the night and got steadily worse until the bailers were unable to keep the canoes from filling, and the paddlers to keep them head on to the mountainous seas. Then Tui Matokano had called on Ligadua for aid, pouring a libation of yaqona to him and promising that if they were saved they would prepare a feast such as had never before been seen on Ono, in his honour, and would make generous gifts to him.

Now Tui Matokano fingered the drum lovingly, and listened to its deep-throated murmur as he stroked it with his hand. Many weeks had gone by since his return, and he had not thought of Ligadua again.

He sat down with his people on the courtyard and joined in the laughter and relaxation that come at the end of the day.

"Who is that?" someone asked suddenly.

They all looked up, and saw a young man emerging from under the shade of the breadfruit trees. He held himself erect and walked proudly towards the king. He was unarmed, but had none of the caution to be expected from a stranger. His eyes flashed fire from beneath beetling brows. With a sinking heart Tui Matokano saw that the young man had only one arm. He strode past the petrified chief and laid his hand on the drum. Then, with a great laugh that rolled and echoed through the clearing, he sprang up into the air and sailed over the tree tops. Under his arm could be seen a faint shadow which had the appearance of a drum.

"It was the great god Ligadua," wailed an old woman; but Tui Matokano shook himself and laughed a little shakily.

"Nonsense. It must have been a dream," he said. "But now I remember that we have not given the feast we promised to Ligadua. Beat the drum to call the warriors together for a meeting, and we will make our preparations at once."

A young man stepped forward, picked up the heavy sticks and struck the drum, but no sound came from it. He struck it again, with a look of amazement on his face, and when it was still silent he dropped the sticks and fled.

Tui Matokano sprang to his feet.

"What is the matter with you, you fool?" he shouted. He picked up the sticks and struck the drum with all his might, but it was silent.

The king turned slowly and faced his people. Their chattering had died down and all was quiet. Then from far away, from distant Tuvana, they heard a muffled roll of a drum they knew to be their own.

Never again did the vesi drum brought from Kabara speak to the people of Ono. It remained silent until it decayed and fell to pieces – the drum they called Sagasagawale, which means "All our work for nothing".

THE MAN WHO WAS USED AS A BALL

FOR many days there had been no rain on the island of Ono. The vegetation had withered, and in the village of Matokano the food had all been eaten. Remembering that the island of Tuvane was a fertile, unoccupied land, the villagers sent a canoe there to bring back provisions. The largest canoe was put into commission, manned with a crew of both men and women.

They reached the island one afternoon, and by dark had loaded a good supply of coconuts into the canoe. That night the crew slept in a hut which had been erected years before for the convenience of those who visited the island, but they slept fitfully, for a strong wind rose during the night. In the morning the waves were pounding on the beach and it was obvious that it would be a rough voyage back to Ono. They debated whether they would remain until the storm died down, but eventually it was agreed that the women should remain on Tuvana, while the men took the coconuts back to their people, whose food would by this time be exhausted. The women could be picked up within a few days.

Amongst the men was one named Tui Liku, unmarried, with an eye for a pretty girl; he was an ingenious fellow, especially when planning anything for his own benefit. He slipped away from the meeting before the discussion was over, announcing his intention of gathering more food before the canoe set sail; but as soon as he was out of sight he hid in the bush and waited for his friends to leave. It was a cunning plan. He intended to explain his absence by saying that he had been lost. He chuckled to himself, imagining the tumultuous welcome he would receive from the young women when the other men had sailed, for he was a general favourite with them.

It was unfortunate for Tui Liku that he had not stayed to the end of the discussion. There were signs that the gale was blowing itself out, and the meeting decided that they would all return home together, both men and women.

The unsuspecting Tui Liku crept to the edge of the bush and peered through the grass. He saw the men emptying the last of the baskets into the canoe and hoisting the sail. So the young man wandered about, leisurely filling his basket with stones and broken coconut shells; then, as the canoe got well away from the shore, he strolled down to the beach. For a moment he was puzzled that there were no women to be seen on the beach, and then the truth dawned on him. They were all in the canoe!

Dropping his basket he raced down to the water's edge, wildly shouting and waving his arms. Some of the men waved back derisively, but the canoe sailed on. Tui Liku's purpose had been suspected by the men, who had suffered at his hands before, and he was left alone on the island.

He spent the day wandering aimlessly to and fro or gathering provisions, and in the afternoon he went inside the hut and lay down to sleep. He was awakened by the sound of voices, and rejoiced to think his people had returned for him. It was dark. He called out, "Here I am – it is I, Tui Liku."

The only answer was a mocking laugh and a babble of voices in a tongue he could not understand. He drew back and crouched against the wall of the hut. A crescent moon was rising and silhouetted in the dim light by the doorway was the ungainly figure of a hunchback. Tui Liku's heart seemed to drop into his bowels, for he realised that this man, and those whose voices he could hear, were demons.

The hunchback stretched out a long thin arm, closed his hand over Tui Liku's arm and dragged him through the doorway. He laughed again, and with the strength of a giant tossed Tui Liku high into the air. Before he fell to the ground another hand caught him and flicked him up again. So began a game such as children play with dawa fruit, but with Tui as the ball. His arms and legs were nearly torn from their sockets, and every part of his body was bruised. Hours went by as the moon sailed slowly across the sky, and to the accompaniment of screams of laughter, the young man was tossed and tumbled from one to another. He seldom touched the ground, for the incredible strength and swiftness of the demons kept him in the air all the time. After many hours, during which the stars spun round in ceaseless gyrations, Tui's senses left him.

When he regained consciousness he found he was lying on the floor of the hut and the sun was high. Groaning, he crept slowly and painfully out into the sunshine, cautiously feeling his bruises. He was too exhausted to eat, but scooped water from a stream to relieve his burning thirst. There was no sign of the demons; but he realised they would return by night and that he must do something to defend himself.

He spent the afternoon gathering logs and building heaps of

The young man was tossed from one to another.

firewood round the hut. In the gathering darkness he set fire to them and for a while sat watching them with satisfaction. He lay down contentedly, and smiled to himself when he heard high-pitched voices raised in anger. But shortly afterwards the smile vanished from his face and he sat up with a jerk, for he heard the sound of water hissing into steam; peering through the flames he saw that the demons had filled banana leaves with water and were emptying them on to the fires. As the flames were extinguished the demons leapt over, seized the unfortunate man, and tossed him out to their friends. All through that night he was tossed to and fro, and at dawn left battered and weary by the hut.

Although he could scarcely keep his eyes open, Tui Liku dared not sleep until he had thought of a place to hide from the demons the following night. He saw a tall coconut palm and climbed painfully to the crown, where he crouched among the leaves. At first he thought he had succeeded. Looking down, he could see the dark shapes of the demons searching for him everywhere. Presently one of them said that he thirsted for the milk of a coconut, and began to climb the tree in which Tui Liku was hiding. The man's eyes stood out in horror as the demon mounted slowly towards him. The head emerged from the leaves, the eyes widened in surprise and delight; then a strong hand shot out and jerked the man from his precarious perch.

He fell sickeningly towards the ground, but at the last moment was caught and tossed back up to the tree top, where he was caught again and thrown far out towards a waiting circle of demons.

The next day Tui Liku was again in a sorry condition, half dead from lack of sleep and bruised body and limbs. He dreaded a fourth night of sleeplessness and bruising. As he anointed his body with oil from the coconuts it occurred to him that if he could separate himself from the demons by water, they would not be able to reach him. He wandered round the shore until he came to a place where a tree grew close to the water's edge. He felled it so that it splashed into the sea. The fallen trunk was still attached by a few strips of bark to the stump, while the head of the tree rose and fell in the waves.

He crawled out along the trunk and crouched half in, half out of the water. When the demons came out of their hiding places, he strained his eyes to see them, and rejoiced as they searched in vain. His eyes closed and, half submerged and cradled in the leaves, he fell asleep. But the leader had discovered the newly cut tree-stump. Boldly he ran along the stem, plucked the sleeping man by the hair and with a scream of laughter threw him ashore, where the others waited to begin their fiendish game. All that Tui Liku had gained was a few hours' respite; by morning, he was barely able to move, so grievous were his bruises.

Fire, air, and water had not protected him from the malicious, playful demons. Tui Liku wished that the earth would open and swallow him up. At that moment he saw the kaiki, the little sand crabs, scuttling across the beach, and a new idea came into his weary mind. He dug a hole, lay down in it and scraped the sand over himself, leaving a funnel through which he could breathe.

In the darkness he could hear the cries of the demons as they searched in vain. The hours were going by, and Tui had drifted off to sleep. He was wakened by voices. The leader of the demons was speaking.

"He has given us the slip," he said. "His people must have come back and taken him away. There will be no living ball game for us tonight. Let us make a feast of crabs."

In his hiding place Tui Liku could imagine the plight of the crabs, as the demons poked in the holes with sticks. Soon there was a yell.

"Sobo! See what I have found! This must be the hole of the king of the kaiki!"

The demon thrust his hand down the hole, caught Tui by the nose and pulled him out. The maniacal laughter of the demons rang out once more, and again Tui was tossed from hand to hand.

The young man was desperate. The demons departed at sunrise, but he felt he could barely survive another night of such treatment. For a long time he lay brooding over his fate, dropping off to sleep and waking again with a start as he realised that he must devise some plan to save himself.

At last he dragged himself out of the hut and cut down five banana trees. He lopped off the foliage and carried the stems into the hut, where he laid them on the floor and covered them with mats, so that they looked like the bodies of sleeping men.

At nightfall he lay down among the stems and fell asleep. He was woken by the sounds of whispering and shuffling feet, and could imagine the demons peering through the doorway.

"Sobo! They have come back again!" one of them whispered. There was a sound of departing footsteps and then silence.

Presently he heard a voice singing. The melody rose and fell and seemed almost to draw Tui's soul from his body, for never before had he heard such wonderful music. He sat up to hear better.

There was a shout of triumph from one of the demons who had been hiding near the doorway.

"Come!" he called. "There are no world-men here, only Tui Liku. If they had been men they would have heard the song, but only one of them has moved. It is another of Tui Liku's tricks."

They rushed inside and handled the exhausted man more roughly than ever before. He was thrown from one end of the island to the other. At daybreak he knew that his last night was approaching. He ached from head to foot and his body was a mass of bruises, while he could hardly hold up his head from lack of sleep.

In his extremity he sought help from the gods, because his own strength had failed him.

Immediately there stood in front of him a stately figure, looking at him with clear eyes. It was Ligadua the One-Armed, a lord of the spirit-world of Burotu, whose special duty was the care of the people of Matokano.

"What is your trouble, my son?" he asked gently. "Why are you so sleepy? Why is your body covered with bruises?"

Tui Liku told him all that had happened to him. The god was angry. He beat on his drum, the celebrated Sagasagawale he had taken from Ono many years before. The demons came running at the summons and seated themselves in a circle round Ligadua, who reproved them so sternly that they hung their heads in shame, and plucked at the grass, promising that never again would they torment any of the people of Matokano.

"Now you may remain here safely until your friends return for you," Ligadua said to Tui Liku. "As for me, I shall return to Burotu."

As soon as he heard the name of the spirit-land, the young man forgot his aches and pains.

"Take me with you," he said eagerly.

Ligadua answered gently, "You do not know what you are asking. I could take your spirit with me, but it might never return to your body. No world-man has ever returned from the land of the gods."

Yet Tui was not to be denied. He begged so long and earnestly to visit the mysterious land that at length the god consented.

"As you desire it so earnestly, you may come, if you will

promise to do exactly as I tell you, and to follow me wherever I go."

They were standing together on the beach, watching the waves roll in.

"When the white waves roll in, Tui Liku, remain where you are. When the black waves come, stand still. The wave that will carry us to Burotu is red, so when a red wave rolls on shore, jump with me, and it will take us to our destination."

The god lifted his voice and shouted.

"*Lele mai mua vesi!*"*

A huge red comber towered over the black waves and the white waves and crashed on to the beach. The god and the man jumped together, and their souls were carried off to Burotu. Tui's body was lifted up and flung on shore, where it remained, spread out on the sand, as his soul made its journey to the island of the gods.

The red sea-canoe reached Burotu.

Ligadua and the spirit of Tui Liku left the beach and walked along a path, which led to the village of the gods.

"Stay here till I call you," Ligadua said. He entered the council house where his father, the lord of all the gods, sat with his chiefs. The king greeted his son affectionately.

"What news do you bring us of the world-men?" he asked.

"I have brought the spirit of one with me," Ligadua replied. "He was tormented by the demons of Tuvana, and when he begged to visit our island I gave my consent."

"It is good," said the king. "Let him be admitted to the council."

Trembling, the spirit of Tui Liku entered the meeting house of the gods. He prostrated himself before the king, and then watched as attendants brought offerings to Ligadua. First there were two young coconuts on a branch, red and fine, such as Tui had never seen before. Then yaqona was made ceremoniously and given to the god to drink.

After the ceremony, Tui whispered in the god's ear. His request was passed on to the king.

"The spirit of this man humbly craves a gift of the red nuts," Ligadua said to his father. The king tossed back his head to show that he consented.

For a while the young man remained in the king's village listening to the sound of singing that stirred the heart even more

---

* *Mua vesi* was chiefly canoe made from red vesi-wood. The words mean, "Bend over towards us a chiefly canoe."

than the song of the demons, and his eyes were round with wonder at the sights he saw as the gods played together.

When the time came to return, the god took Tui Liku with him again to Tuvana. The nuts were borne safely across the ocean and planted at Mataniwai, where they continue to flourish.

Four times the spirit of Tui Liku accompanied Ligadua to Burotu, and each time he returned with a gift. The second time it was a coconut tree which is short-stemmed and bears a prolific crop; a third time it was miji, the little bird that haunts the coconut groves; the fourth time it was qai kula, the great almond.

But on the last occasion the spirit of Tui Luki was disgusted to find that while his body was lying on the sand, just out of reach of the waves, a sandpiper had pecked out one of his eyes.

"I cannot enter that mutilated body," he exclaimed; but Ligadua was firm.

"You must go back to your body," he said. "If you do not, your soul will be lost, and without a home for ever."

Then the spirit of Tui Liku entered his body and remained at Tuvana until his people returned. They laughed at him a little, and gave him a new name, Matadua, which means the One-eyed One.

But the dilios, the sandpipers of Tuvana, remember his earlier name. To this very day, as they search for food on the sandy shore, they cry, "Tui Liku, Tui Liku."

THE ROLLING HEAD OF THE GOD

ULUPOKA, the god of Ono and of Lakeba, took part in a great battle of the gods. It must have been a terrible sight to see them attacking each other; a sight that no mortal man might endure. Ulupoka's head was severed from his body, but as the gods are deathless, the head was endued with immortal life. It fell to earth and, as he was an evil and malicious god, the appearance of this ghostly head was always a sign of ill omen, bringing sickness and death to any to whom it appeared.

The head usually came at dusk when men were sitting with their families. A sudden coldness in the air would precede its coming. Sometimes it entered into baskets which had been thrown away, and if a man saw a basket rolling over and over on the ground when there was no wind, he would know that Ulupoka was there.

But to those who were doomed, the head entered their houses. They would hear a snarling sound. The head would bounce across the threshold and roll over and over, with grimaces that were even more horrible as the head turned this way and that, sometimes upright, sometimes on its side or upside down. Nearer and nearer it would come, until at last it reached its victim. The god's mouth would open, and its teeth would bite the man's toe. With a terrible shriek that rang through the village, it would roll out of the house and disappear; and in a short time the man would fall sick and die.

THE LADY OF THE SKY

The men of Uruone were planting the dalo in the water-terraces when they heard a noise in the sky which sounded as though some object were rushing towards them. They looked up and saw a dark speck which grew larger and larger as it approached. When it was overhead they could see that the strange creature was a goddess. She fell from the sky in front of them, right into the Na Kele Kele stream. The water surged over the bank, and as it began to run back into the bed of the stream, a large grey rat climbed out and ran along the path that leads to Daku.

"It is Adi Mailagu," someone exclaimed. "The Lady of the Sky has come to make her home with us."

They looked at one another fearfully, wondering what would happen next. The rat had disappeared, and there was nothing left to do but to finish their work and return home.

The following day word was brought to the village that the rat had been seen, and had spoken to men at Udu. Shortly afterwards strange stories began to circulate, which proved that a goddess had indeed come to live among men, and that she had an evil spirit. She took many forms: sometimes she showed herself as a beautiful young woman, at others as a withered repulsive old crone, and again as a grey rat. She made her home in an ivi tree, and woe betide anyone if he made a noise as he passed the place.

Soon children began to fall sick, and it was discovered that Adi Mailagi had stolen their shadows, putting them in her palm-leaf basket and carrying them away. We know this is true because some of the shadows escaped and came back to their owners; but if they did not return the children died.

The greatest danger came to the young men of the tribe. To them Adi Mailagi appeared as a young woman of beauty so ravishing that they left their houses and gave themselves up to her embraces. After that she would leave them, and they would wander about in a daze, with no thought except of the goddess. Eventually they would be taken sick, and lie on their mats until she came to them and gathered up their souls, like a fisherman catching fish with a net.

It was only the most handsome men whom she afflicted. To women, and to men who did not appeal to her, she appeared as an old hag, dirty and unkempt. Occasionally she injured them, if she was in a spiteful mood.

On one occasion the men of Uruone were bringing a large drum which they had made from the wood of the vesi tree from Daku to their home at Udu. It was heavy, so when in the late afternoon, they reached a place where the path climbed over a steep hill, they decided to leave it there and return for it in the morning. Shortly after they had left, a young woman happened to go past, and noticed the drum sitting on the ground with the drumsticks beside it. She picked up the sticks and beat the drum, listening admiringly to the sound as it rolled across the valley. Adi Mailagi sprang out of a nearby tree and pushed her down so fiercely that her leg was broken.

It was well for Gulia Meli that the goddess had not taken a liking to her. Many tales are told of those whose spirits she captured; many are the stories of those who escaped from her. There was Tui Merike who was riding on his donkey at dusk near Uruone when the goddess appeared from behind a tree and pounced on him, shouting, "Where are you going?"

The poor beast was trembling with fear and Tui Merike knew he was in the presence of Adi Mailagu. He urged his donkey and galloped down the path with the hag close at their heels. Over hill and valley they flew until he came to Mualevu, where she left him, calling after him, "You have escaped, Tui Merike, but it is only because of your speed."

Again, another man came round a bend in the road and surprised the goddess. She was in the form of an old woman, sitting on the ground, while from her mouth her red tongue lay across her knees and trailed on the ground. The man was on her before he realised she was there. For a moment he was petrified as he saw her tongue coil itself up like a snake and disappear into her mouth. She shrieked and dived into the water, emerging later at a considerable distance.

It was necessary to appease this goddess. The priests carried wood to the ivi tree where she had made her abode, and made a fire. When the goddess smelled the smoke she emerged as a rat. She jumped across to the branches of a nearby makosoi tree and sat down, answering questions which the priests put to her. Afterwards she descended to the ground, where she allowed the priests to rub her fur until it glistened, and to feed her with tit-bits. The rat goddess became the oracle of the tribe, and would warn them when one of their principal men was about to die.

It was in her manifestations as a woman that Adi Mailagu did so much harm. No one could touch the goddess, whether she appeared as a beautiful young woman or an ugly hag, but in the rat form she was more vulnerable.

It was in modern days that Tui Uruone went with his young men and cut down both the ivi and the makosoi tree; but Adi Mailagu escaped, and it was Tui Uruone who died.

Where is she now? Who can tell? But beware the young woman who comes to embrace you at night, for she will imperil your soul.

GODS WHO FOUGHT FOR THEIR WOMEN

ALTHOUGH the gods usually had as many women servants as they needed, the acquisition of a wife was often a difficult task for them. The daughter of a god was the only fitting spouse for a god, and such women were scarce. Ravovonica-kaugawa, the powerful god who lived at Rewa, in Viti Levu, had long wished for a mate who was beautiful in appearance, wise in council, and generous in disposition. He had visited the dwelling places of other gods of Fiji, and of the women he had seen, none pleased him so well as the daughter of Rokouma, the god of Naicobocobo, in Vanua Levu. In the long hours of the night the vision of this attractive goddess filled his mind, driving sleep away, and transporting his spirit to a mountain top of delight. Blended with these thoughts were intolerable longings. Unfortunately he was not friendly with Rokoua, and doubted whether he would be well received if he asked for the young woman in marriage.

Such cravings cannot be denied indefinitely, no matter what obstacles have to be overcome. He asked his friend the god of winds to accompany him on a visit to Naicobocobo.

"Why?" asked his friend. "Are you tired of living in Viti Levu? Are you in such a hurry to make your departure for Bulu, the land of everlasting life?"

"I know as well as you do that it is the place whence spirits leave for Bulu," Ravovo answered impatiently. "I want to take some of Rokoua's women-folk to keep me company. It is not right that he should have a wife and children while I have no one to share my sleeping mat or to talk to when the nights are long. Will you help me?"

"Anything you say," the wind god agreed, "especially where women are concerned."

The two friends set sail. They crossed over to Vanua Levu and followed the coast until they reached the western point of the island. They threw the anchor overboard, and waited expectantly for Rokoua's people to welcome them with gifts of food. It was a long wait. The sun sank, and rose, and sank again, but still they saw no sign of gods or men. It was evident that Rokoua knew their intentions and had forbidden his people to extend the usual welcome to visitors.

But when have gods or men been able to control their women-folk? Every morning the land breeze brought the smell of luxuriant vegetation, and with it a more persuasive scent, overpowering, heady, langourous. It was the scent of the lovely young woman Naiogabui, the daughter of Rokoua. Some bond of the spirit united her soul with the soul of Ravovo. Without ever having seen him she fell in love with him. She told her women to spend the day catching fish and to cook them in the evening. It was the third night that the canoe had been anchored off the village of Naicobocobo, and Ravovo had become reconciled to his disappointment.

It was a dark night. The wind god lay fast asleep in the stern of the canoe. Ravovo sat brooding in the bow, his face in his hands, his head bowed, his heart sad and heavy in his breast. There was a phosphorescent surge in the black water, and suddenly to his startled gaze there appeared the woman of his desiring, bearing gifts of cooked food. He helped her into the canoe, and long before the meal had been eaten they knew that each was made for the other.

"Let us pull the anchor up and set sail at once," he whispered.

"Not yet," The young woman Naiogabui replied. "Tomorrow night."

"Tonight," Ravovo pleaded.

"My dear one, I would gladly come with you now, but I have my reasons. For a long time my friend Naimilamila has been planning to escape, and this will give her the opportunity she has longed for."

"Who is Naimilamila?" Ravovo asked suspiciously.

"She is the youngest wife of my father. She was taken by force. She does not love him and he has no affection for her. He only keeps her to comb his hair and scratch his scalp when it is itching. It is no life for a lovely young woman. You would not spoil my happiness by denying my friend's, would you?"

"No," Ravovo said, "I would deny her nothing, and you even less, bright light of my life. Hurry back to your father now lest he suspects what we are doing. But do not delay tomorrow. Every hour that you are away will be an eternity."

She pressed his hand, slipped silently into the water, and swam back to her home.

The day passed by as slowly as any day in the memory of Ravovo; but night returned at last and the two gods strained their eyes in the blackness. Again there was a swirling of phosphorescent light. Ravovo put out his hands and drew the young woman out of the water and into his arms. But the scent was not that of his loved one. He drew back and peered at her.

"Who are you?"

"I am Rokoua's wife."

"Where is Naiogabui?"

"She is coming. Quick, pull up your anchor and hoist the sail. There's no time to lose."

Ravovo caught her by the shoulders and regarded her with a piercing look.

"Why should we hurry?"

Naimilamila shivered.

"Please believe me. The god of Naicobocobo will miss me, and he will set out in pursuit in his war canoe filled with armed warriors."

A hand appeared on the gunwale of the canoe and Naiogabui climbed over the side.

"It is true, my dear. I heard shouting from the house of the god and saw lights among the trees. Please hurry."

Ravovo woke his friend. The wind god raised the sail while the anchor was being pulled in, and the canoe glided across the lagoon, lifted its prow to the big waves that ran through the break in the reef, and sped southward through the night. The wind hummed in the sail; before dawn they were at Rewa, and the gods took the women ashore.

Rokoua had indeed embarked in his canoe, the Vatutulali, which took its name from his drum, which was so large that it could be heard all over Vanua Levu. Everything that Rokoua owned was larger than those of mortal men or even gods. It took ten men to lift his spear and club, and the canoe settled deeper in the water when they were put on board. By the time it left the lagoon Ravovo's canoe was out of sight, but the god of Naicobocobo knew very well who had taken his wife and daughter.

He did not attempt to sail direct to Rewa, but landed at Nukuilailai. The canoe sailed close in to the shore. The crew lifted their paddles and the Vatutulali glided to a standstill. Rokoua bridged the gap between the canoe and the shore with his spear and walked across. His club was already in his hand. He pulled his spear towards him and waved his men away.

He walked along the beach, his head bent in thought. "Ravovo will be waiting for me," he reflected. "I would gladly split his skull with my club, but he will have hidden the women where I cannot find them. I shall have to use stealth and cunning. What kind of form can I assume that will not make the god suspicious?"

He lifted his eyes and saw an old woman walking towards him. She was carrying a basket of cooked dalo and pudding. As they passed each other, Rokoua changed bodies with the woman. She knew nothing of the change and walked on without a word. Leaving his spear and club on the beach the god hurried onwards, his back stooped, his face and body thin and wrinkled, and with long white locks falling over his face. In his hand was the basket of food.

He came to the house of the god in Rewa and went up to the door. His daughter was standing there. She looked at the old woman and enquired, "Who are you?"

"I have come from Monisa," the woman said. "I have brought you a present of food."

"Come in," said Naiogabui with a smile. "Sit down and rest."

The two young women and the older one whom they thought of as a friend, sat on the mats eating food and talking.

"You are strangers here?" the old woman asked.

"Not really. We belong to Ravovo, but we have only been here a few hours."

"Then you won't know where the best places are for a swim. Come, and I will show you."

They got up and followed the old lady, who led them along the beach and round a rocky point. The huge weapons that belonged to Rokoua were lying on the sand. The girls' eyes opened wide, and they shrieked. The old lady snapped her fingers. Her body straightened and expanded into the enormous form of the god who was their husband and father. He stooped down, picked up his weapons, and drove the terrified women in front of him until they reached the Vatutulali. Once again a bridge was made of the spear and the canoe sailed back to Naicobocobo.

Ravovo was nearly distraught when he found that he had lost his lover so quickly. He followed the footprints of the three women along the beach. When one of these changed to the larger prints of a man – one who was of gigantic stature – everything became clear to him. In his rage he launched his canoe and sailed for Naicobocobo once more. The canoe was beached at the village and Ravovo and the wind god rushed into Rokoua's house; but righteous indignation was no match for the strength and wiliness of Naiogabui's father. The two gods were quickly overpowered and made prisoner in a small tumbledown house. Indignities were heaped on them; under strict guard they were forced to look after Rokoua's pigs. The men treated them with contempt, but the women were sorry for them and smuggled tasty morsels from the god's food to them whenever they had an opportunity.

An invitation to a feast at a village some distance down the coast was received, and everyone went to it, dressed in their best clothes and in holiday mood. Even Ravovo and his friend were taken. It was easier to keep watch over them in this way than to leave guards behind at Naicobocobo. But there was no feasting for the gods of Rewa. They were told to guard the canoes while the others went ashore, but it had been forgotten that Ravovo's friend was a god of the wind.

"What can you do?" Ravovo whispered urgently as soon as they were alone. His companion shivered violently.

"What do you want?" he asked.

"Wind! A wind to frighten Rokoua and his friends."

"A wind there will be."

When the feast was over and everyone embarked again, the canoes set sail for home. As soon as they were well out from the reef a northerly gale sprang up. The waves hissed over the sides of the canoes, but by bailing and paddling ceaselessly they managed to reach Naicobocobo.

As usual the men went ashore, leaving the women to bring off the loads of gifts. Ravovo and his friends were ordered to help them. They contrived to get the other women out of the way while Naiogabui and Naimilamila remained aboard. The two gods went aboard the two canoes, each taking one of the young women with him.

"An east wind," Ravovo said quietly. The wind god raised his arms, the wind changed direction; the sails, which had not been lowered, bellied out in a tight curve, and the canoes turned and sped down the coast to Rewa.

Once again Rokoua had to take the initiative if he was to bring back his wife and daughter and retain the respect of his people. His own canoes were gone, but Ravovo's canoe was still lying on the beach at Naicobocobo. There was no hope of catching the fugitives at sea, because the wind that the wind god had conjured up went with him, leaving a flat calm behind. It was a long, tiring journey for Rokoua's paddlers, but eventually they reached land and their god stepped ashore. He stumbled as he left the canoe, and dropped his club. It fell with a thud that could be heard from one end of Viti Levu to the other, and the noise warned Naimilamila.

"Be careful, Ravovo," she said. "That was Rokoua."

"Nonsense," the god laughed, "it was a peal of thunder in the hills."

"No, you are wrong. It was Rokoua's club falling down. Believe me I know."

"Well, if it was Rokoua we will be ready for him. My men are waiting."

"You won't know him when he comes. Remember how we were deceived by the old woman who came here last time?"

"If any old woman comes here now, she'll get the fright of her life."

They waited a long time. No old woman came near Rewa. In fact no stranger came to the village except a young girl, carrying a gift of shrimps, crabs, and dalo.

"Excuse me," she said politely. "My mother sent me with this food as a gift to the god, for we have heard that he was nearly starved while he was kept prisoner at Naicobocobo."

She was so young and fresh, with a bright flower in her hair, and such a charming smile that she was invited into the house.

"Sit down," said Naimilamila. "Have you come far?"

"It was a long walk," said the girl as she crossed her legs and sat down on the mats.

Naiogabui was watching her very closely. She frowned and drew her husband outside.

"It is Rokoua," she whispered urgently.

"Nonsense!" the god exclaimed. "It is a girl who has come from the inland regions, from a little village far up in the hills."

"It is Rokoua," Naiogabui persisted. "He sat down like a man, not like a woman. Look at him while Naimilamila is talking to him."

Ravovo peeped through a crack in the wall. The girl was certainly sitting very awkwardly. He watched her more critically and saw that she gestured as a man.

"Are you sure?" he asked his wife.

"Quite sure."

"But I must be certain. If it is really a girl I would never forgive myself if I hurt her."

Naiogabui was exasperated.

"If you don't believe me now, you'll never be able to trust me. You can hear her answering Naimilamila's questions if you listen, and you'll see that she knows nothing about the hills of Viti Levu.

She doesn't even speak like a woman. Listen, Ravovo: if you don't kill him now, he will kill you. But I won't be here to see it. I am going away now."

She walked away quickly. Ravovo took a step after her, hesitated, turned back and rushed into the house, brandishing his club. The girl sprang to her feet. She took the stance of a fighting man, caught up a spear that was leaning against the wall and faced Ravovo. The girl's legs thickened, her arms grew lean, corded with muscles, the body began to change to that of a man. Ravovo looked at the changing form with relief and anger in his heart.

"Out of the way, Naimilamila!" he shouted and swung his club with all his force, splitting Rokoua's head before the god could touch him with the spear.

Others came running at the noise, and when they looked down and saw the huge body of the god of Naicobocobo lying on the ground wearing the tattered dress of a young girl, they were so infuriated that they beat his head to pieces.

"You are brave now," said Ravovo with a smile, "when you have nothing to fear."

His arm was round Naiogabui, and when he looked round he saw that Naimilamila was equally happy in the encircling arms of his old friend the wind god.

THE GOD OF THE SUMMIT OF GAU

THE reasons for quarrels between husbands and wives are as many as the leaves on a tree, or as the fish in the sea. Fortunately the winds blow, the waves roar, and the leaves and the fish are swept away. But while tempers are frayed it is better for husband and wife to be apart.

At least, that was what two men who lived on Gau thought when their wives quarrelled with them and went off by themselves to take part in the feasting and games at Namuanaira.

"Now we can have a good time together," one of them said with a sigh. "What shall we do?"

"Let's have our own feast. There's plenty of fruits and vegetable here, but we need meat. They've taken the pigs with them, but perhaps we can find some land crabs."

They looked amongst the trees and had drawn close to the shore when suddenly they saw a tall stranger in the distance. They hid behind a tree to see what he was doing in their neighbourhood. Against the background of the blue sea they saw him leave the shadow of the trees and stand on the white sand. With starting eyes they saw him shrug off his arms, and heard him say, "Go and wash yourselves."

The hands stretched out their fingers. On their moving tips they crossed the beach and plunged into the water. They were followed by the legs, which moved independently but as though they were still attached to the body; and after them the man's torso rolled down to the sea and vanished into the water. Only the head was left.

Presently the various parts of the body emerged and joined themselves together. The head climbed up the body and seated itself on the neck, and the tall figure walked swiftly between the trees, making towards the mountains. The two villagers, following at a safe distance, eventually saw the stranger walk up to a kauri tree near the top of the mountain and disappear within it.

"This is a wonderful thing of magic," one of them exclaimed. "Surely he must be a god."

"There is no doubt. See how tall he was, far beyond the stature of an ordinary man. And his head – and arms – and legs!"

"If he is a god, then we must pay our respects to him. We shall remember this place and this tree. It is late. Soon the sun will set, and we shall be food for evil spirits if we stay here. When the sun returns let us come back and tell him we will be his servants."

They gathered a large yaqona root and took it to the kauri tree next morning. As there was no sign of the god, they sat down and clapped their hands rhythmically, until he appeared, towering over them.

"What do you want?"

"We have brought this kava root to you as a gift."

"Why have you done that, little men? Do you think I am a god?"

"We know you are, sir."

"How do you know? Just because I am taller than you does not mean that I am a god."

"Sir, we were looking for crabs among the trees yesterday and we saw your head sending your body and limbs into the sea to bathe. Then we knew that you were a god."

The giant smiled at them. "It was given to you to see what no others have ever seen. But why have you come to me now? Do you want something in return for the yaqona?"

"No, sir. Our wives have left us for a while, and all that we want is to be your servants."

"If your hearts are clean and you have no thought of gain, then you may be my servants. Prepare the yaqona now and we shall drink together. Meanwhile I shall arrange for a meal to be prepared."

He looked up through the foliage of the tree into the sky and called out, "Spade!"

Immediately a spade came tumbling down and began to dig the earth without hands to wield it.

"Wood!" called the god, and dry timber plummeted from the sky and fell in the trench that the spade had dug.

"Stones!" called the god, and there was a clattering sound as they fell on the wood and spread over the trench that the spade had dug.

"Fire!" called the god, and a sheet of flame kindled the wood and heated the stones that lay in the trench that the spade had dug.

"Flesh!" called the god; but no flesh came from the sky. The god looked at the men with a calculating eye.

One of the men distrusted the way the god was looking at them, but the other said eagerly, "I will be honoured to do what you ask."

"Good!" the god replied. "You must trust me, and I will see that whatever happens you shall come to no harm. Now, my good servant, jump on to the hot stones in the trench."

The man did as the god said, and fell prone on the red hot stones.

"Leaves!" called the god. The tree trembled, the branches waved madly in the still air, the leaves fell like rain, fluttering down on to the man's body, completely covering the stones and the wood, and filling the trench that the spade had dug.

"Spade!" the god called for the second time, and the spade got to work covering the leaves with earth and patting it until it was smooth.

The other man and the god sat down together and watched the mound, from which little puffs of steam escaped from time to time. Presently the god got to his feet and said, "The meal is ready." The spade came up to him and scraped the soil and leaves away. Underneath there were several pieces of savoury meat, which they ate.

More of the leaves were scraped away, disclosing several layers of mats made of tapa cloth ornamented with striking designs. When the last one was lifted out, the body of the faithful servant was seen lying on the stones. His body twitched, his eyes opened, and when he saw the god he jumped to his feet and knelt in front of him.

"You are indeed a faithful one," his master said. "You may go home now, but when you need me I will always be by your side."

He put several of the mats into his arms and dismissed the two men. All through the night they discussed the strange events of the past two days. The one who had drawn back when the god asked for his allegiance lamented his cowardice and indecision.

"Forget all about it," his friend urged. "All that really matters is that I have a pile of mats to give my wife when she returns. I will give one to you, in order that you may make peace with your woman too. We may never see the god again, but at least he has promised to come to us when we need him."

"Well, if we may not see him again we might as well go and enjoy the games before they are over."

They came to the village where the games were being held, but no one took any notice of their arrival.

"We are important men. We are servants of the god of the mountain. They should revere us," said the cautious man.

"Very well," replied the other. "We will show them!" He lifted up his voice.

"Listen, all you people. My friend and I wish to give you a feast."

At these bold words the men and women gathered round and laughed at them.

"That would be very nice. But where's your food? Where's the oven?"

"I will show you."

He held out his arms and called as the god had done, "Spade!"

A shout of astonishment went up as a spade fell from the sky and began to dig a trench. The cries of surprise continued as wood and stones and fire were conjured out of nothing; but while the stones gradually turned a dull red colour, someone asked again, "But where is your food?"

"There is your chance," whispered the man who had volunteered previously.

"Yes," said the other. He addressed the crowd. "We promised a feast and we have come prepared. Watch!"

He stepped on to the stones and lay down. Several of the people rushed forward to restrain him, but his friend stopped them.

"He told you to watch. Obey him!"

The trench was covered over by the spade and everyone waited in silence. It seemed a long time until the feast was ready. It was with apprehension that the people stripped off the earth and leaves. Underneath they found an ample supply of food cooked to perfection. But they did not want to eat it. Tapa cloth was lifted out, and there was the man who had entered the oven, alive and well. His skin was oiled, his eyes sparkled, and he was clad in gorgeous robes so that he looked almost like a god himself.

"Tell us what you have done," everyone cried. "Something mysterious has happened. What is the meaning of these strange things?"

So the tale was told for the first time, as it has been related hundreds of times since and at the conclusion all cried:

"Great is the god of the mountains! We will all be his servants and he will be our god. Great is Tui Delai-Gau, the god of the Summit of Gau."

THE GOD WHO TURNED HIMSELF
INTO A RAT

HAVING heard what a beautiful place the island of Bau off the coast of Viti Levu was supposed to be, Qurai, a god of Somosomo, on Taveuni had a great desire to visit it. He had no canoe, but one of his chiefs cut down a large bamboo for him. The god changed himself into a rat, shouldered his club, and crept inside the hollow stem. The chief pushed it off, shouting directions and encouragement to Qurai.

The journey was a long one. A perverse spirit seemed to enter the cylindrical boat, which rolled round and round in the waves, forcing Qurai to run round the sloping surface to prevent himself from being flung backwards and forwards. It drifted from one island to another, never touching land, but continuing its erratic course towards Bau. The food stores had long been exhausted, and Qurai despaired of ever reaching land. A huge wave upended the bamboo, tipping him into the sea, and his club floated out of his reach; he feared his last moment had come, so he scrabbled frantically with his paws, trying to get a grip on the smooth surface of the bamboo. It was tossed about even more violently and caught in the grip of the surf.

Bruised and battered, with the sound of breaking water roaring in his ears and the whole world a welter of white foam, Qurai was flung head over heels over the reef into the smooth water of a lagoon.

Coughing and spluttering, he raised his head and tried to find where he was. A large hand reached down, scooped him out of the water, and dumped him into the bilge of a canoe. Qurai shivered violently. He was still shivering as the canoe was beached. The same hand picked him up and carried him to the cooking house of the chief. For four days and nights the soaked rat shivered on the hearth. The cold had shrunk his magic powers and he was unable to turn himself back into his true shape.

As he sat and shivered he was conscious of a stir and bustle in the village. Huge piles of food were being brought to the cookhouse, and enormous ovens were being made to hold them. In the distance he heard singing, and soon the ground began to shake with the thunder of feet stamping in unison as songs of welcome were chanted, and the dances in honour of a distinguished

LEGENDS OF THE GODS 63

visitor began. He listened to the cooks as they chattered, and was mortified to learn that it was the god from Vuna, another village on Somosomo, who was being entertained so lavishly.

His anger drove away his fear. He was not able to change his form, but his voice came back. The cooks looked round in astonishment as they heard a thin squeaky voice which said: "I am Qurai, the paramount god of Somosomo. Take me to your god at once."

One of the cooks threw back his head and roared with laughter.

"Look!" he said, as soon as he could control himself. "This castaway rat is trying to talk."

They bent down to hear what he was saying.

"Take me to your god. At once, you fools."

The cook picked him up in his hand.

"Let's do what he wants," he said to the others. "I'm sure the god would like to share the joke with us. Fancy this miserable half-starved rat thinking he is the god of Somosomo!"

"You'd better leave him here in the meantime until our god has had a talk with the god of Vuna. You can take him tomorrow," one of the older cooks advised.

Qurai spent the night huddled in a corner chewing his whiskers with rage. He could hardly wait for the morning when he felt he would be able to convince everyone of his importance.

When the time came he was picked up unceremoniously by the scruff of the neck and taken before Omaisoroniaka. The god of Bau was a majestic figure, twice the size of a man. His skin was oiled, and as he sat on a mat facing the god of Vuna, he towered over everyone else. Little Qurai smiled as he heard what the great god was saying. The yaqona bowl passed between the two god-like figures, but Omaisoroniaka was coming to the end of his speech.

"And so my brother of Vuna," he was saying, "you see how advantageous it will be for you to pay tribute to me. You will retain your independence, and all you need to do is to pay tribute to me once a year and to acknowledge me as your overlord. In return I will protect you against your enemies, feed you in time of hunger, and at all times I will call you my brother."

"Your kindness overwhelms me," replied the god of Vuna. It was difficult to detect the note of sarcasm that lay beneath the polished words. "This island of yours is fertile and pleasant, and you are indeed a god among gods. But I too am a god, and unworthy though I may be, and poor my little island, nevertheless

I am the god of my people. If I paid tribute to you they would no longer regard me as their protector. I would rather be the god of Vuna than a lesser god of Bau. These are my words. Great is my gratitude to you for your brotherliness. Although it is of your great kindness that you have made this proposal to me, I know that deep in your heart you would rather see me as a fellow god than as one who bowed before you in servility. I return to my own people knowing that there will always be brotherhood and respect between the people of Bau and the people of Vuna."

Omaisoroniaka stood up and put his hands on the other's shoulders.

"I think you are mistaken, my friend, but I respect your . . ."

He whirled round.

"What is that squeaking sound?" he demanded.

The cook stepped forward with a broad grin and held out a woven mat on which a thin rat was sitting.

"Are you daring to joke with your god?" Omaisoroniaka thundered.

The smile faded from the man's face.

"Oh no, my lord. This is the principal god of Somosomo. At least, that's what he claims, and I thought you would like to see him."

The two gods stooped over the rat, and slowly the grim expressions on their faces changed to a smile. The little rat god was standing on his hind legs shouting with all his might, but all they could hear was an agitated squeaking.

"I am the chief god of Somosomo," the voice shrilled, "and like my friend I reject your proposal. Never, never, never will I be the vassal of the god of Bau."

Omaisoroniaka patted the rat on the top of his head with his enormous finger.

"Never mind, little rat, you can go home now. I am sure the god of Somosomo will be glad to take you in his canoe."

Qurai was handed over to a servant who took him down to the canoe and deposited him gently on top of a pile of provisions.

It was not until the canoe reached Qurai's own island that he recovered his self-confidence and his normal shape and stature.

Some time later the god of Bau made a return visit to the god of Vuna. He came with a large retinue, determined to press his earlier demands, but his host was ready for him. During the night he got his men to pour water over the path that led to his house, until it was slippery and dangerous to walk on. He waited until

Omaisoroniaka raised the matter of overlordship again. As soon as his guest began to speak of the superior force and beauty of Bau, he turned away and walked towards his house, avoiding the path. The face of the Bau god was suffused with rage and the veins stood out on his forehead. He clenched his hands and took a hasty step towards his retreating host.

Alas, he stepped on the slippery path – his feet slid from under him and he came down heavily on his back. In a flash the god of Vuna had turned and was kneeling heavily on his stomach, his hands round his throat, his eyes glaring.

"So you would dare to try to force me to subjection in my own home!" he shouted. "It is I who am the lord of all the islands. If you do not acknowledge this, now, before all your people, I will squeeze the life out of you."

He loosened his grip. Omaisoroniaka gasped for breath and said hoarsely, "It is true. You are the overlord. I will pay tribute."

"What will you do?"

"I will not make food for you, nor will I bow down before you, but I will give you my club, and I will tell all men that you are the chief of gods."

"It is well. We are brothers; but I am the elder brother."

He released his grip and stood up, knowing that there would be peace between them.

After that, the people of Vuna were always respected and welcomed by the people of Bau.

But what of the god of Somosomo, self-styled lord of the isles, lord of Taveuni, and overlord of the god of Vuna? His degradation was never forgotten. When visitors went to Bau from Somosomo, even though they regarded themselves as superior to those of Vuna, they were forced to lower the sail of the canoe long before they reached the island and to paddle ashore in a sitting position, for to stand would have cost them their lives. On landing they were required to give the shout of reverence that is a mark of respect to a chief, and to do it with a trembling voice in imitation of the quavering voice of the rat god. For four days they might dress only in shabby garments, and even when this period was over and they were allowed to clothe themselves gaily, as for a feast, they walked about doubled over with their hands on their breasts.

When they were met by a man of Bau, he would laugh and say, "Ho, ho! Has Qurai been set free yet?" And to this they would reply, "Yes, sir, Qurai has now been set free."

CHAPTER III
RATU MAI-BULU THE SNAKE GOD

HOW THE ISLAND OF VIWA WAS BUILT

THE god of growth and fertility, Ratu Mai-bulu, lived in the Yasawa group of islands with the god Raivuki, who was responsible for the changing of seasons. One of their attendants, Rainima by name, had served them long and faithfully, but he had become weary of working for others and went to his master Ratu Mai-bulu with a request.

"My people and I have served you for many years, lord, and now we would like to have a place of our own."

"You have been my faithful attendant, Rainima," said the god. "You may form a settlement wherever you wish in this island of Waya."

"Thank you, lord, but that is not really what I meant. We would like an island of our own."

Ratu Mai-bulu shifted on the coils of his shining body, and his tongue flickered in and out. If a snake could be said to smile, there was amusement in his face and voice. The snake head waved slowly from side to side.

"Alas, Rainima, we have no island to give you."

"But there are many islands in the sea . . ."

"Not belonging to us, Rainima. Yet there is something we can do for you. How would you like to build an island for yourself and your friends?"

"How could we do that, lord?"

"Do you see the coral reef there, far out at sea? If you like to bale out the water, I will help you to raise it from the bottom of sea."

Rainima gave a broad grin. It was not for nothing that his name meant "the one who bales".

"Thank you, lord."

He wasted no time in telling his people what they were to do.

"I want you to gather stakes and tie them together. Lash them well, because we are going to make a fence. When you have done, take them down to the canoes in bundles. If we get them done before midday we shall be able to leave at once."

"Where are we going, Rainima?"

"To the coral reef you can see out there."

They stared at him in disbelief.

"What good can it do to put a fence out there? Do you want to build a fish fence?"

"No. It's for something else. Hurry up and get to work and I shall show you."

There was a great deal of speculation and not a little grumbling, but eventually the canoes were loaded, and the little flotilla set sail for the reef. On arrival Rainima ordered them to hammer the stakes into the coral in a large circle, while he began to bale the water out of the reef. When night fell the canoes returned to Waya, leaving the solitary figure silhouetted against the moon, stooping and straightening itself, throwing the water away from the reef. All that night he toiled, and the next, and the next. Sometimes he despaired of ever completing his task because the water flowed back as quickly as he baled it out; but three months after he had begun, the reef was nearly dry. It gave a lurch, and Rainima's heart nearly stopped beating. It rose slowly above the sea, the water cascading from its sides like a waterfall.

Tired as he was, Rainima leapt into his canoe and sent it speeding across the water to Waya.

"Oh lord," he called to the Snake God, "I give you thanks for your gift of this island of Viwa to me and my people. Now we will scatter earth over it, that the land may be fruitful and become a place for men to live."

It took a great deal of persuasion to induce his people to fill the canoes with soil and convey it to the new-born island, but as the pile grew larger on the firm foundation of coral, they became excited, and were as anxious to build new houses there as Rainima was. But before this was done he had one more request to make of the Snake God.

"What is it now?" Ratu Mai-bulu asked.

"Water!" said Rainima. "There are no springs or rivers on my island, and the rain soaks straight into the soil."

"You must depend on the rain for your supplies. I have raised the land for you, and now you must prepare the soil and plant seeds. When the trees grow I will cause them to fruit, and then you can think of water. Here is a dawa seed; plant it first of all, and come and tell me when it is grown."

Rainima left him.

"How silly to plant just one seed!" he thought. "I will take a bag full of them, and then we shall have plenty of fruit."

Before long, houses had been built of timber taken to the island by canoe, and everyone waited anxiously for the plants to grow.

Rainima had planted the god-seed of the dawa in front of his house and it grew quickly and became a great shady tree, but all the other seeds died or lay dormant.

The people complained again.

"We need water, Rainima. That is why the trees won't grow. The Snake God looks after his own, but the others need fresh water. There's nothing to hold it here, because it sinks through the coral."

"Don't worry," their leader said. "I'll go over to Waya to the source of the water where it springs up from the ground. That must be the seed of fresh water, and if I bring it here it will well up from the soil just as it does on Waya."

He spread his arms out as though they were wings and flew into the air. He circled the little island he had made with the help of the god, and flew across the sea to the mother island, Waya. It took only a little while to reach the spring. He cupped his hands and drank of the cold, clear water. He had nothing to carry it in, but he made a vessel of dalo leaves, filled it to the brim and flew back.

Ratu Mai-bulu saw him flying overhead and guessed what his servant was doing. He was angry because Rainima had not asked him to help. He picked up a coconut and threw it, knocking the leaf bowl out of his hands. Rainima was startled. He grabbed it, but unknowingly caught the coconut instead and flew away with it in a panic. When he arrived at Viwa his people abused him for bringing back a useless coconut and threw it away; but the shell put out roots and a stem and grew into a fine tree. It bore nuts which fell to the ground and in turn grew into trees which covered the island.

But long before this happened, Ratu Mai-bulu had visited the island to see how the settlers were faring. They flocked round him, asking him to bless their trees and make them fruitful and, above all, to give them a perpetual supply of water.

"Had you come and asked me I would gladly have given you water," the god replied, "but you thought that my servant Rainima could grant you what you wanted. You did not put your trust in me, even when I raised your island out of the sea, but gave all the credit to Rainima. If I had not lifted up the land he would still have been baling water out of the reef. He failed you when he promised to give you water, and this is your punishment. Only one thing will I do. will I make your coconut trees fruitful. When you have drained them and eaten the contents you can keep them as cups in which to store rain water for drinking; but for bathing you must use salt water, you and your children and your children's children, until the island of Viwa sinks back to its home in the sea."

THE CHIEF WHO CHALLENGED A GOD

ON the island of Bau, Koroika, an important chief, was openly scornful of the gods.

"But surely you believe in Ratu Mai-bulu, the snake god who lives in the cave nearby?" he was asked. "Everybody knows that he is a powerful god. Many of us have seen him for ourselves."

"I have never seen him, and I don't believe he is a god at all," said Koroika. "Oh, maybe there is a big snake there, but to say it is a god is ridiculous. I shall go there to find out for myself."

They tried to dissuade him, but he was a proud man and not to be turned from his purpose.

"I won't waste my time," he told them. "I am going fishing, so I shall paddle along the shore near the cave and when I've made a good catch I'll pay a call on your mythical friend Ratu Mai-bulu."

He leaped into his canoe and sent it surging through the water until he came to a good fishing ground. He lowered the anchor, and before long the pile of fish in the bottom of the canoe was proof that the place was a good one for fishing.

"Now for Ratu Mai-bulu!" he said to himself, laughing as though it were a great joke. He paddled towards the dark mouth of a cave in the cliff. When he reached it a small snake glided out and looked at him. Koroika was surprised that this should happen at the very moment of his arrival, and even more so when the snake spoke.

"Who are you? What do you want?" it asked.

In a rather subdued voice, which his people would not have recognised, the chief said, "I have come to see Ratu Mai-bulu. Are you that great god?"

"No, I am his son."

Koroika reached down and put several of his largest fish on a boulder in front of the cave.

"Please accept this fish as an offering to the god," he said.

The snake bowed its head and disappeared into the cave. Presently an even smaller snake came out. The chief's courage was returning, and when he saw the tiny snake, scarcely bigger than a large earthworm, he said scornfully, "Surely you are not Ratu Mai-bulu! I am Koroika, and I have come to make sure that you are not a god."

"I am the grandson of the great and noble god Ratu Mai-bulu," piped the little snake in a high-pitched voice. "I don't know whether my grandfather will see you or not."

Koroika tossed a fish to him contemptuously.

"Let me see your wonderful grandfather or I won't believe in him. Tell him that Koroika is waiting to see him, craving an audience."

The snake disappeared into the cave, leaving the fish lying where the chief had thrown it.

A third snake began to emerge. Koroika blinked. Never in his life had he seen such an enormous snake as this. His head filled the mouth of the cave, and when he lifted it up and loop after loop of his enormous body came forth, he towered above the little man down in the canoe.

"I must prove whether he is a god," Koroika murmured to himself. "This is an enormous snake; but is he a god?"

He fitted an arrow to his bow and fired it at the snake's body. Digging his paddle in the water he turned his canoe and with a few frantic strokes sent it out of reach. God or no god, he knew it would not be wise to stay within reach of such a head and such fangs.

Ratu Mai-bulu coiled his body loop on loop, but even so his head soared up almost to the top of the cliff. He stared so steadily down at the chief that Koroika felt uneasy. Little twinges of fear began to pluck at his heart.

When the snake spoke the voice was soft and melodious.

"Nothing but snakes; nothing but snakes," it said almost sadly.

Koroika shivered. He paddled home, not daring to turn round and look at the god, but above the splash of his paddle and the sound of the water rippling past the prow of the canoe he could hear the soft voice repeating, over and over again, the mysterious words, "Nothing but snakes; nothing but snakes."

By the time he reached his home his confidence had begun to return. As he walked up the beach he was greeted by his people, who wondered that he had returned alive after his impious words.

"If he is a god, he is very feeble," Koroika told them. "Oh yes, I saw the great snake, and it spoke to me. But I don't really think it is a god."

He went into his house and called for a meal, which was brought to him in a dish. He lifted the cover and to his horror he saw that the dish was filled with black snakes. Their fangs flickered in and out as they crawled out of the dish. He sent them spinning through the open door. His people were watching him closely, and he tried to appear unconcerned.

"Bring me a drink of water," he cried. He tipped up the earthenware jar, but more snakes slithered out. Koroika shuddered.

"I am tired," he said. "I will lie down and sleep. Prepare more food for me when I wake." But no sooner was he lying on the mats than he felt snakes crawling over him, smothering him, wriggling underneath his body. He sprang up and rushed from the hut. The snakes were all over its floor, and with a sob of relief he reached the open air and slowed his pace to a dignified walk. As he passed the temple he heard a priest talking excitedly.

"Ratu Mai-bulu is angry," the priest was saying. "Someone has wounded him in the hand with an arrow. What shall we do? If he cannot be appeased he will destroy us all, for he may never return. Then the trees will no longer blossom or fruit."

The last shreds of pride and unbelief fell away from the chief. He went up to the priest, confessed what he had done, and told of the punishment that had already begun.

"What shall I do?" he asked, "I have offended the god. I will give all I have if I can win his forgiveness."

"That is what you must do," the priest said gravely. "Take everything you value most to the god, and ask whether he will forgive you for your impiety."

Koroika loaded his canoe with his most costly possessions, with food and with flowers, and paddled back to the cave. Ratu Mai-bulu said nothing, but listened carefully. His eyes were sad. When Koroika was finished he bowed his head. The chief took this as a sign that the god was pacified. The offerings lay on a flat rock in front of the gigantic snake, and the chief returned to his village, a humble man who would never again question the existence of the gods or challenge their power.

THE BATTLE OF THE GHOST AND THE GOD

ON Cicia Island all men lived in fear of Ratu Koli. Koli was a great warrior of the Walakewa tribe, fearless of his enemies, proud and quarrelsome, and he had brought the men of Na Vuwai into subjection.

At night the Na Vuwai men gathered secretly in their huts, whispering together and plotting revenge. It seemed simple when they had each other's support, and there was no one to overhear; but in the daytime they remembered that Koli was skilled in the use of all weapons and had many men to support him, and their courage evaporated.

In the end it was a Na Vuwai woman who was responsible for throwing off the yoke of the Walakewa tribe. She kept taunting her husband, accusing him of cowardice, until in desperation he went to the village of Lagatea, where Ratu Mai-bulu was the god. His example inspired his friends, who crept behind him in fear and trembling. When they came to Lagatea they found that a new house was being built for the god, and that the last post was being lowered into the hole in the ground.

Shivering at their own audacity, the Na Vuwai men advanced and poured yaqona into the post-hole as an offering to the god, asking him to fight against Ratu Koli.

They returned to their homes and waited. Three days later news was brought to them of Koli's death. The first night he had been troubled by dreams, and when woken the next morning he was in a fever. In spite of all that was done for him the fever mounted. On the third day the chief sat up and cried, "I know you, Ratu Mai-bulu! It is you who have done this evil thing to me. Beware! I am Ratu Koli, and I am subject neither to man nor god."

No sooner had he uttered these words than he fell back and died.

A weight was lifted from the souls of all the Na Vawai people. Songs were heard in the the evening, and men walked with lighter hearts and no longer dreaded the wrath of the chief. Soon they forgot what it had been like to live in oppression, and when the time came for the memorial ceremony on the hundredth day, they all went to take part in it. A dead chief was of no greater consequence than a dead animal, and everyone could join lightheartedly in the performance of the last rites.

Before these were over, the boy who had been put in charge of the canoes, which were drawn up at a little distance on the beach, came running up to say that one of them had floated off by the rising tide. It was night, but there was bright moonlight. The young men raced off, and managed to secure the canoe. They were sitting on the sand after their exertions when they heard a rustling in the bushes. They turned round and were terrified to see Ratu Koli stepping out into the moonlight. His war paint stood out clearly in the silver light, and in his hand was his oiled club.

The young men huddled together at the sight of the apparition. The ghost cried hoarsely. "I see you, Ratu Mai-bulu! Now you have met your fate!"

From the opposite direction the god appeared, terrible to look at. He stared contemptuously at the ghost of the dead warrior and said, "What is the insignificant creature I see here? Do you dare challenge me? Who are you?"

"I am the spirit of Ratu Koli, whom you caused to die. On guard, Ratu Mai-bulu!"

The ghost and the god thumped the ground with their clubs until it shook, and fire brighter than moonlight flashed from their eyes. They rushed together, and the sound of the falling weapons clashed like thunder.

Presently Koli's club crashed on to Ratu Mai-bulu's shoulder, forcing the god to his knees. He held his club over his head, to protect it from the blows that were raining down on him.

"Pardon!" he cried. "Spare me, Ratu Koli. I confess that I have done wrong. It was because your people sought my help that I sent the fever to you. But you are stronger than I. If you let me go, I will be their god and yours. I will protect you and send nothing but favours to you. Only let me return to my temple in Lagatea."

Ratu Koli leaned on his club, breathing heavily.

"No! I do not trust you, Ratu Mai-bulu. It is my will that you go to the Na Vuwai people and live with them, but you may not return to your temple. The new house will remain empty, that all people may know that I am stronger than you and have imposed my will on yours."

Ratu Mai-bulu bowed his head. As the young men watched, the fighters disappeared, the place of combat was a moonlit emptiness,

They rushed together and the sound of falling weapons crashed like thunder.

RATU MAI-BULU THE SNAKE GOD

and the only sound was the hissing of the waves on the sand and the rustling of palm leaves in the evening breeze. Even the sand lay unruffled where the supernatural beings had fought so fiercely.

The men returned, and told their people what had happened. As the ghost of Ratu Koli had commanded, the temple at Lagatea remained empty. Ratu Mai-bulu lived always in fear of Koli in the village of Na Vuwai, which changed its name and became Maibulu, to prove that Ratu Koli, powerful even in death, had forced the god to do his will.

Maibulu town is the name of that place to this day, but at the time of feasting they call it Na Vuwai, to remind them of the far-off days before their god was conquered by a ghost.

CHAPTER IV

DAKUWAQA THE SHARK GOD

THE BATTLE OF SHARK AND OCTOPUS

DAKUWAQA the Shark God was the most restless and therefore the best-known of all the monsters that guarded the reef entrances of the islands. He was headstrong, fearless, and jealous of all other reef guardians. He spent a good deal of his time fighting with them, or trying to find and challenge others whom he had not met.

His quest took him to the islands of Lomaiviti. It did not take him long to subdue the guardians of this reef in the group, so he set out for Suva. For the moment he was sated with battle, but when he was challenged by a local monster, the old fire returned to the Shark God, and they circled each other warily. Dakuwaqa dashed in and seized the guardian in his strong jaws. To and fro they struggled, raising great waves which rolled into the mouth of the Rewa River, and flooded the valleys for many miles inland. In the end the local god paid for his temerity, and Dakuwaqa swam onwards with his jaws open wide in a broad grin.

As he drew near to Beqa he met his old friend Masilaca, who was also a Shark God.

"Have you ever been to Kadavu Island?" Beqa asked him.

"No."

"Afraid?"

Dakuwaqa felt the blood rushing to his head.

"If we had not known each other for so long I would show you whether I am afraid or not."

"I know, I know. I was only teasing you. I thought you might be interested." He glanced slyly at his friend. "I have heard it said that the monsters there are stronger than you – but of course that is nonsense."

He had to struggle to maintain his balance, for Dakuwaqa did not stay to hear any more, and the water swirled fiercely round Masilaca as Dakuwaqa turned and sped towards Kadavu. As he drew near the reef he heard a deep voice calling to him from the shore.

"I am Tui Vesi, the guardian of the Vesi tree. My work is more important than yours. I would gladly join battle with you, but I cannot leave the land nor you the sea. Yet if you go further down the coast you will find a reef guardian who will prove worthy of your attention."

To his surprise he found himself brought up with a jerk.

What a monster it proved to be – a giant octopus, which anchored itself to the coral with four of its arms and held the others loosely on top of the water. Dakuwaqa adopted his usual tactics and rushed towards his opponent with his mouth open wide and teeth gleaming like shining white knives.

To his surprise he found himself brought up with a jerk. Two tentacles coiled round his body, another kept his tail from moving, and a fourth arm slid round his mouth and gradually forced the gaping jaws together. The middle tentacles gripped tighter, almost squeezing the life from him. They were bands biting deeply into his flesh. The shark felt that in another moment the life would be squeezed out of him. With a huge effort he wrenched his mouth open against the squeezing tentacles and for the first time in his life he begged for mercy.

"If I let you go, will you protect my people when they go fishing?" the octopus asked.

"Yes, I promise."

"Will you keep them safe from sharks at all times?"

"Yes, yes, I promise."

The octopus released him, and Dakuwaqa kept his promise faithfully. The fishermen of other islands must guard against sharks continually; but from Kadavu the canoes go out with men laughing and singing, following the phosphorescent wake of Dakuwaqa, knowing no fear. He has become their protector.

THE LAND THAT WENT TO SEA

THE chief Ratu Vouvou was in a gay mood, so he ordered his people to make a feast at the mouth of the Naseakawa River. It was not long before a procession of villagers was on its way down the track to the coast, carrying heavy loads of food, and chattering gaily as they thought of the good time they would have. On arrival at the river mouth they divided into groups, some preparing the fresh vegetables and fruit and putting them in heaps on the grass, others making the ovens ready, and others killing the pigs which had been driven down from the chief's village.

"Here, children, you can help," one of the men called when the preparations were well under way. "We have cut up the pigs, but the meat needs to be washed in salt water. Take it down to the beach and wash off the blood."

It happened that Dakuwaqa, the Shark God, was cruising round the coast of Vanua Levu at that time. All the reef monsters had been subdued and now he had nothing to do but swim lazily round the coast, dreaming of his many victories and thinking of ways of filling his capacious belly. Even that took little effort, for he had a companion whose duty it was to swim close to shore and report any tempting morsels to its master.

This messenger, who was a large saqa, was swimming close to where the fresh water of the Naseakawa River mingles with the ocean, when suddenly every nerve in his body began to quiver. He could smell blood, and when he opened his mouth he could taste it – fresh and intoxicating to a fish.

"My master must know about this; but first I must find where it comes from," he thought. He turned into the current of fresh water, which was tinged with pink, but when he reached the mouth of the river he lost the scent and found that the water was crystal clear. He cruised backwards and forwards, and finding no further trace of blood came to the conclusion that the source must be somewhere up-river. As he swam upstream against the current the children, who had finished washing the meat, saw his fin cleaving the water, and ran excitedly to tell their elders.

"There is a saqa swimming up the river," they shouted.

The men were equally excited.

DAKUWAQA THE SHARK GOD

"Just what we need to make the meal perfect," they exclaimed, "but how can we kill it?"

"If it has gone upstream it must come down again," said Ratu Vouvou, who had come down to see what all the shouting was about.

"There is nothing up there for a fish as big as a saqa. I wonder what he went there for! But look, the tide is falling and soon it will be too shallow for him to get out to sea. Take your spears and stand in a line across the river. Don't let him get past you."

The men waited for some time. Then twenty voices cried together, "Here he comes!"

They could see the fin racing down the ebb tide. The saqa tried to get past, but wherever he turned the men jabbed him with the points of their spears. They were not strong enough to kill or even wound the fish, but they kept him from escaping into deep water. Ratu Vouvou waded towards him and with a mighty blow of his axe struck off his head. It was washed out to sea, while the men lifted the body out of the water and carried it ashore to add to the meat that was cooking in the ovens.

By midday Dakuwaqa began to wonder what had happened to his saqa. He swam towards land in the direction his messenger fish had taken, and on reaching the Naseakawa River he was taken aback at seeing its head being swept out to sea in the current of fresh water. The Shark God swam close to the shore. Lifting his head out of the water he heard the sound of singing, and saw people dancing, and the remains of a feast on the ground. Quietly he swam to the shore on the other side of a point of land, walked over the sand, and turned himself into a tree with shady, pendant branches.

While the men and women were dozing in a mid-afternoon lethargy, the boys and girls went down to the beach to play and swim. They soon noticed the tree in a green expanse of grass, growing where no tree had ever grown before. They ran and told the chief, who came down to see the unusual sight for himself.

"I have never seen anything like this before," Ratu Vouvou said, "but we must not disdain the gifts of the gods. Come, my people, the time of feasting and dancing is over, and now we can rest under this shady tree."

His people moved over to the tree, and Dakuwaqa waited until they were all asleep again. He gently detached himself from the land and, like a little island, the grassy patch and the shady tree that were really Dakuwaqa the Shark God, floated out to sea.

The ocean swells rose and fell, lifting the island and the sleeping men and women, then sinking again into the hollows. One of the branches broke off with a sharp crack and splashed into the water where it turned into a shark. The chief woke up with a start and called to his people.

"Wake up! Wake up! See what is happening!"

They sat up and watched the branches falling one by one into the sea, or rolling over on the grass until they reached the water. As soon as they touched the sea they were transformed into sharks, which swam round the little island, turning over on their backs and displaying their gleaming teeth. The land and the denuded tree shuddered under the impact of their bodies. The people feared that the soil and the grass would dissolve under their feet, leaving them at the mercy of the sharks.

Only Ratu Vouvou realised that Dakuwaqa had taken the shape of a tree. He caught the trunk in his hands and braced his body against it.

"The fault was not ours, O Dakuwaqa. We were not to know that the saqa was your messenger. What must I do to save my people?"

The tree spoke. "Is your heart sorrowful towards your people, Ratu Vouvou?"

"My heart is strong, Dakuwaqa, and they are my people."

"By strength and by sorrow will they be saved. Look to the land and be comforted."

The chief looked, and raised his voice in a shout. "Be ready!"

A bar of sand had appeared among the breakers and was advancing towards the floating island, which was beginning to shake and crumble to pieces before the attack of the many sharks.

"Hold on! Hold on tightly!" said the tree. The muscles in the chief's arms had grown rigid and the veins stood out on his forehead, but he held on to the swaying tree as the sandbank touched the island. The men and women leaped on to the causeway and ran back to the mainland, but Ratu Vouvou remained alone, still clinging firmly to the tree trunk.

"The island is going, Ratu. The sharks are closing in. Is your heart still strong?"

The chief looked down. Now the only part of the island that remained was the tiny patch of grass where his feet were planted, and the sandbank had disappeared.

"My heart is very strong, Dakuwaqa," he said. "Receive the thanks of a chief for your clemency."

He felt the trunk slipping downwards, sliding through the water, changing its shape as it went. Bending his knees he sprang into the air, thrusting the tree away from him. It was a mighty leap as though a stone had been thrown in the air, or an arrow shot from a bow.

His last glimpse of Dakuwaqa was of a giant form in the shape of a shark that dwarfed the fish that swam amongst the floating debris; a moment later he stood safely on the shore in the midst of his own people.

THE SHARK GOD

THE islands of Lau cover many sea leagues. For long the people of the northern Lau Islands paid tribute to the lords of Cakaudrove on Vanua Levu, but those of Lakeba in the southern islands refused to acknowledge their overlordship, because they belonged to Dakuwaqa, the Shark God.

Tokairahe was the son of the god Tui Lakeba and the goddess Liku Cava. There was great skill and no little magic in Tokairahe's fingers – the fingers that fashioned the enchanted hooks which made him master of all the fish of the sea.

Only one fish had the temerity to resist the hooks of Tokairahe. It was Dakuwaqa, the enormous Shark God, who was the king of all fish. He realised that his reign was at an end unless he could get possession of these hooks.

He left his home and swam through the sea until he reached the island of Lakeba. For three days he waited off shore, drifting in with the tide, lurking in the shadows, and taking refuge in the shadow of the reef when the tide ebbed. Nothing that happened inside the reef escaped him, and on the third day his vigil was rewarded.

He saw Tokairahe come out of his house, naked except for the shimmering glory of the shell fish hooks which he wore round his neck. The young man ran into the water and struck out towards the reef.

Silently the Shark God sank towards the bottom of the lagoon, gliding like a shadow deep below the surface. He turned over and saw the body of Tokairahe suspended above him. The huge form of the Shark God was like a sea spirit. Before Tokairahe was aware of him the Shark God caught the necklace in his teeth, lifted it over the young man's head and, with a flick of his tail, sped off towards the open sea.

His triangular fin was raised high above the water like a sail as he set out for his home in the north. Tokairahe gave a cry of grief, for his shell necklace was precious to him. His friend, Tui Vutu, heard the cry and when he saw the dark fin cutting through the waves, he realised what had happened. He changed himself into a bird and flew after the Shark God.

The Shark God had a good start in the long race, but Tui Vutu's wings were strong, and his love for Tokairahe great. Slowly he

DAKUWAQA THE SHARK GOD

gained on the huge fish, and just as it was taking refuge in its home in the sea off Vanua Balavu, he caught up with it. He plunged downwards, snatched the necklace, and returned to Lakeba, where he returned it to his friend.

Tokairahe was grateful. He conferred the rank of Mataivalu Kalou on Tui Vutu, so that he became the leading man among his people.

It was because Tokairahe had overcome the Shark God Dakuwaqa that the people of Lakeba proclaimed their independence.

Many years passed by. The white man came to the islands of Fiji, of Lau, of Lakeba and Vanua Balavu, of Moala and Ono, of Rotuma and all the other far-flung islands and said that the lords of Lau should no longer pay tribute to Cakaudrove; but the people of the northern islands of Lau still maintained the customs of their fathers, and carried gifts to Vanua Levu.

So it happened that Akuila Toro, the chief of Mualevu, sailed in his schooner to take gifts to Tui Cakau. While in the Somosomo Straits a gale sprang up and the vessel foundered. Toro and his men began to swim to the distant shore. Before they had gone far, a huge shape appeared out of the water. It was Dakuwaqa, who had recognised his own people and come to protect them on their long swim.

They climbed wearily on to the reef and gave thanks to their god; but amongst them was a Tongan who had no allegiance to the Shark God. He cursed Dakuwaqa, insulting him with the name that means "a corpse prepared for the pot".

Many months later, when the Tongan returned to his own land, he was eaten by a shark – for Dakuwaqa never forgets an insult.

THE SHARK WHO SWAM AWAY FROM HOME

EVERYONE knows that Dakuwaqa, the Shark God, lived long ago in the seas of Fiji. This story is about a young shark who was one of Dakuwaqa's sons, He decided to go away from the other sharks and to live by himself, so he swam off alone, up a small tidal stream that flowed into the sea not far from the island of Bau.

After he had left there was great consternation amongst the sharks, for no one knew where the son of Dakuwaqa had gone. They searched everywhere, but found no trace of him. The news spread to all the nearby villages that Dakuwaqa's son was gone.

There was one small village not far from the stream where the young shark was hiding. Little did the people of that village imagine that this shark of noble birth was their near neighbour.

One sunny morning a man and his small daughter went down to work in the food garden. It was some distance from the village, so they had a long way to go. They walked along a path with trees and grass on either side. The man was carrying his digging stick, while the little girl carried a basket on her back, for she intended to bring home some green cooking bananas for her mother to cook for their evening meal.

They come to a little stream, and crossed it by a bridge made of the trunks of two coconut palms lying side by side. As they crossed they looked down into the water, and there they saw the young shark swimming up the stream.

"Father, father," the girl cried, "come and look at this big eel." Her father ran back quickly to see what the girl was looking at, and said, "Oh yes – you wait here. I'll go back home and get a spear to kill this eel."

The man was skilful at spearing eels and he knew that he would not miss his target. He raised the spear, ready to plunge it into the stream, when the shark turned over on its back, and he discovered that it was not an eel at all.

What was even more surprising was that, as soon as he saw it, he knew by the markings on its belly that it was the lost son of Dakuwaqa. He drew back his hand, glad that he had not thrown his spear, and ran back with his daughter to the village. Both of them called out in loud voices, and the people came rushing to see what was the matter.

"Dakuwaqa's son!" the man gasped. "In the stream."

"Tell us about it," cried the people.

As the man got ready to tell his tale the old people prepared yaqona, filled the coconut cups, and poured some out on the ground as an offering to the shark. Then they all solemnly drank in turn, saying, "Dakuwaqa's son, go home! This is not a suitable place for you!"

They kept this up for several hours, until the yaqona was all finished. Then they went back to their own houses and slept soundly, for they were sleepy after all the excitement and the drinking of yaqona.

As soon as morning came the men rushed down to the stream to see if the shark was still there. And there he was – but he was not alone! There were dozens and dozens of other sharks, great and small, so that the stream was packed from bank to bank. As the men watched, the sharks all turned and swam down the stream together till they were out of sight.

The incantations that had been chanted in the village that night had taken effect, and all the sharks of the sea had come to take the naughty one away, back to his true home.

After they had gone there was a wonderful change in the little stream. Whereas it had been muddy and shallow before, now the water was deep, and blue in colour. Since that fateful day it has been a lovely, deep, blue stream, and those who visit the village are always told that once the son of the famous Dakuwaqa lived there for a short time.

CHAPTER V

ISLAND VOYAGES AND DISCOVERIES

HOW THE MEN OF LIVUKA CAME TO LAKEBA

ON the island of Bau, the people of Livuka lived on the high ground, while the people of Butoni had their village on the beach. Both tribes were subject to the Lords of Bau. One day the men of Livuka went on to the reef, where they speared a large fish. After long struggling they killed it and dragged it ashore. Such a fish had never been seen before; even its name was not known, but its flesh was sweet and good to eat.

"Why should we take such a prize to the Lords of Bau?" the people asked each other. "They are strong men and we fear them; but if we eat the flesh of the fish that the gods have sent us, and tell no one, they will know nothing of it."

"Eat then," said one. "Talk less and eat up. The deed will be done and forgotten."

Even the women of Livuka kept their tongues still, and all was well, until one of the boys took a long slender bone from the unknown fish and made it into a bow. The young men of Bau came down to the beach and saw the bow shining white in the sun.

"The bow!" they shouted, "Where did you get it? What is it made of?" The boy was frightened.

"It is the bone of a fish," he said.

"What fish?" they asked. "It is too big for any fish's bone."

"It came from a fish we caught. We speared it by the reef, and ate the flesh for many days. See, there is my mother, Nabuna. She is carrying the roe in her basket."

The young men of Bau hurried home and told what they had learned to their elders. They were angry because they felt they had been wronged by the men of Livuka. They gathered their weapons together and set out to attack them.

In the village everyone was frightened.

"Why were we so foolish?" they said. "Why did we eat the great fish? If we had given it to the Lords of Bau we would not have incurred their anger.

The Lords of Bau advanced on the Livukan village, but behind them the sea began to stir. It swelled up like a hill, and a huge wave surged up the hillside and through the trees. When they advanced, it followed them. When they stood still it lapped at their heels. The warriors looked at each other uneasily, and then at their priest. As they watched him the god entered into him, and he fell to the ground and threshed to and fro in a convulsion. The men gathered round him and waited until the god spoke through him.

"Do not kill the men of Livuka." The words came slowly and clearly from the priest's mouth. "Let them live. I will send them away to a new land. Let them prepare their canoes and gather their possessions together. The people of Butoni will go with them and we shall never see them again."

"It is well," said the Lords of Bau. "We shall let them live."

Then the wave slid back down the hillside, and the peoples of Livuka and Butoni began to prepare their canoes for sea.

Far away at Lakeba the king looked proudly at a large piece of cloth which had been made for him. It had been laid out on the grass to bleach in the sun. He said to his daughter, Lagi, the Sky Lady, "I am going to bathe. Look after my cloth for me. If it rains, take it inside the house so that it will not spoil."

Lagi said, "I shall do so."

When the king had gone, Lagi looked round the sky. There were no clouds anywhere.

"I shall lie down in the shade and sleep," she said. But while she slept, angry clouds drifted across the sky and turned to rain, which pelted down and ruined the cloth.

When the king learned what had happened, he was angry.

"Idle, useless daughter," he stormed. "You cannot be trusted." He thrashed her until he was tired, and drove her out of the house. Lagi went down to the beach, weeping bitterly. She gathered empty coconut shells into a heap and tied them together. As the tide crept up the sand she sat on the coconut raft, which was lifted gently by the rising tide and carried out to sea.

For two days and nights the trade wind drove the raft across the waters, and the tears coursed down Lagi's face as she thought of her home, and her father, and the friends she had left behind.

Then she heard the beating of wings, and looked up to see a mighty bird flying overhead. It circled round her, then settled on the raft. Lagi was afraid, and burrowed down amongst the coconuts to hide.

"What shall I do?" she thought. "If I stay here I shall die. I will fasten myself to the bird, and then I may be carried safely back to land."

In much trepidation she tied herself to the breast feathers of

She heard the beating of wings and looked up to see a huge bird flying overhead.

the bird. Presently it rose and flew onwards, carrying Lagi with it. It was so large and strong that it did not even notice her weight. All day it flew onwards, and all through the night. At dawn it came to the island of Kaba and alighted. Lagi untied the cord that fastened her to the feathers and climbed down to the ground. The bird spread its wings and flew away, leaving her alone in an empty land.

The sun rose, and far away on the sea she saw a tiny speck, which gradually came closer. It was a canoe, and on board there was an old man, a chief of the Livuka, who was coming to Kaba to gather up his fish snares. He saw the Lady Lagi walking the beach. She was tall and majestic, and he thought she was a goddess.

His canoe grated on the sand. He sprang out and bowed before her.

"Who are you?" he asked, "Are you a god? Spare my life."

Lagi smiled at him and said. "You are the god. I am but a woman, and you have come to save me. I am Lagi, the daughter of the lord of Nayau, who lives at Lakeba and is a great king."

"Lakeba?" said the old chief, wonderingly. "I have never heard of that place. Tell me where it lies."

"You cross the sea toward the sunrise," she answered, and told him how she came to be on this lonely island. "Now I wish to return to my father."

"The gods have indeed sent you to me," the chief answered. "I will take you back to your home. I am a chief among the dwellers on the hill at Bau. The Lords of Bau are angry with us and are driving us away from their land. So you will come with us first, and it may be that the gods will take us to Lakeba. You must trust me. If they see you, my people will know that you are a stranger, and they will kill you. But I shall hide you until we leave."

She embarked with him on the canoe. When they got close to Bau he lowered the sail and wrapped the king's daughter in it. On arrival at the beach he lifted the rolled sail with Lagi inside, put it on his shoulder and carried her to his house, where he hid her in the loft above the fireplace.

She remained there for several days, until the people were ready to leave. In the meantime the old man had been hard at work building a wall round the deck house of his canoe.

It was the morning for departure. The old man rolled Lagi in the sail once again. He carried her down to the canoe and put her in the house.

"Listen, my people," he said. "One of our gods will accompany us on our journey into the unknown, and will guard us by night and day. I have put the god in my house. When you pass by, you must turn your heads away and lower your eyes, for it is death to look on the god."

Thus when they had occasion to pass the deck-house, the people crept along on their hands and knees, lest they should look over the fence unawares and see the dread appearance of the god.

At last the canoes put out to sea watched by the Lords of Bau. A fair wind sprang up, and on the second day the canoes came to Koro. It was a good land, and it satisfied the men of Butoni.

"We shall stay and make our homes here," they said. "There are fish in the sea and fruit on the land. This is the place for us and our children."

The men of Livuka left them there and sailed on until they came to Vanua Balavu. Many of them were tired of sailing and dreaded being wrecked by storms.

"Let this be our home," they said. "Why should we keep on sailing, when we do not know where we are going?"

The old chief stood up. "No," he said. "The gods do not wish us to stay here. They will take us to a better land."

Secretly he was disturbed. That night he entered the house and asked Lagi, "Where is this land of Lakeba of which you have told me? We have sailed for many days and have not seen it."

Lagi reassured him. "Do not let your soul be small," she said. "Tomorrow before the sun sinks we shall come to an island. It is called Cicia, and that is the border of my father's kingdom."

As she had promised, the canoes reached the island of Cicia the following afternoon.

During the night the canoes lay off shore. In the morning the old chief led Lagi out of the house, and before the eyes of his wondering people took her ashore. There they met some of the women of Cicia, who greeted them without knowing who they were. But amongst them was an old woman who at one time had lived at Lakeba.

"That beautiful woman is like the Lady Lagi," she said to herself, and she went up to the women of Livuka.

"Tell me, is not that the Lady Lagi who is with you? I had heard that she was dead."

The women laughed at her. "We have never heard of any Sky Lady," they said. But still the old woman was not satisfied. She came closer and peered at the king's daughter until she was convinced.

"It is you!" she cried joyfully. "You are alive. You are our great lady whom we have mourned."

She scrambled to her feet and ran up to the village, shouting, "The Lady Lagi is alive! She has come back to us! She is here with us on our beach."

The chiefs and all the people came running down from the village, and when they say that it was indeed the Lady Lagi, they received her with great joy and honoured the people of Livuka who had brought her back to them, and gave them many presents.

After this, the king's daughter was taken to Nayau, and from there the canoes set sail once more until they came to Lakeba, where they landed at Waqka-Calaca. Five men of Livuka went on shore, talking loudly, as chiefs do when they are together.

"Look at these strangers! They must be chiefs from a land of chiefs!" said the men who were working in the plantations, and they followed them to the village. The men of Livuka went on boldly and asked, "Where is the king's house? Where dwells the Lord of Nayau?"

"Hush!" said the women of Lakeba. "Our king is asleep and must not be disturbed."

The five men laughed, and said, "We have come a long way to see him. Let him be wakened at once."

By this time the king had been wakened by the noise. He came out and sat down.

"Who are you! Where do you come from?"

"We are from Bau," they replied, and told him about the great fish, and how they had been driven out by the lords of their land.

"This is an amazing thing," the king said. "We thought Lakeba was the only place in the world, and now we learn that there are far distant places where other men live. Tell me why you have come to Lakeba from your fair island; for you have enlarged our minds and told us that there are other islands where you might have lived in peace.

"We have brought your Lady Lagi back to you," they said. Then the king was troubled in his thoughts.

"This cannot be true. You mock me, for we have eaten the death feast for our daughter, and our eyes are dry after weeping."

"If it is not true, O King, you may put us to death."

"Then you must be gods!" exclaimed the king. "You have come from Bulu the spirit world, to bring me news of my daughter who is assuredly dead."

"Again we tell you: she is alive and well, and is longing to see you. She is in the house of the god on a canoe at Waqka-Calaca, and if you will receive her in peace, we will bring her to you."

"It is enough; I am satisfied. Let it not be this day nor the next, but four days from now. We will prepare a great feast and rich gifts for the people who have restored our daughter to us."

On the fifth day the canoes were brought up to the beach in front of the king's house. The men of Lakeba sprang into their small canoes and joined their hands. Lagi stepped across them, walking over a bridge of hands until she came to the shore, where a long strip of cloth had been laid out for her to step on.

Attended by the men and women of the village, followed by the children, who danced the dance of spears and sang the song of the god, the Lady Lagi came into the presence of her father, who received her with the greatest joy.

The feast lasted many days, and many were the presents and gifts of land that were made to the men and women of Livuka. When the feasting was over they settled on the new land and lived at peace with the people of Lakeba, sharing the spoils of the sea with them, knowing that this was the country to which they had been brought by the power of the god.

WHY ONO IS FAR AWAY FROM LAKEBA

When the people of Livuka came to Lakeba, they lived at peace with the king and his followers for some time, but there came a day when the two tribes quarrelled.

"This in no place for our children!" a Livuka chief exclaimed. "This land is too small to hold us all. I say that some of us, men and women and children, must sail away in our great canoe, and the gods will give them another land, where they may dwell in peace."

So a selected company boarded the great canoe and sailed away over the sea until they reached Oneata. It was not a land that the gods had willed for them. They sailed on to Vatoa, but again the gods did not speak. They climbed the highest hill and looked across the empty plaza of the ocean.

"Alas!" they said, "we have come now to the end of the earth. We have nowhere to go."

They went down to the shore and danced the spear dance.

In a hollow tree near by lived two gods. They heard the noise of feet and the clash of spears, and put out their hands to see what was happening. They were not noticed by the dancers, but there was a man left on board the canoe who saw the heads appear out of the tree. He was a leper who had not been allowed to join in the dance. He looked at the heads for a long time, and then called to the dancers, "Ya, ya! Come here!"

Some of the young men came to see what was troubling him, and when they learned what he had seen, the boldest amongst them took ropes and crept up to the hollow tree. Signalling to their people to go on with the dance, they threw rope over the tree trunk, and as soon as the gods put out their heads the noose settled round their necks and was dragged tight.

"It is forbidden to the gods to see the dance of the spears," said the young men. "For this you shall die."

"No, no," the gods pleaded. "Spare us, and we will be the gods of your house."

"We have no houses, nor any need of gods to protect them," they boasted.

"Then we will be the gods of your canoe, and direct you in your sailing."

ISLAND VOYAGES AND DISCOVERIES

"We have sailed many leagues without your help."

"Then we will be your gods of war, and lead you in battle."

"We want no gods to fight our battles for us. We men of Livuka are invincible."

The gods conferred together.

"Do not kill us," they said, "and we will bring you to the land of your desiring."

The people gathered round them eagerly.

"Where is this land?" they demanded.

"It is called Ono. It lies behind the meeting place of sea and sky, but we can show you the way. Take us aboard your canoe, hoist your sail, and by tonight you will be there."

The gods were pulled out of the tree trunk, trussed securely, and taken into the canoe, with their feet pointing to the bow. The sail was hoisted, and while it was still light, an island appeared on the horizon.

"It is Ono, the land of our desiring!" shouted the people.

The wind blew steadily, but hour after hour went by and the island was still no nearer. It retreated steadily before them.

"It is the fault of the gods," the leper said sudddnly. "I have been watching them. They have been kicking with their feet and thrusting the island away from us."

The men were angry and belaboured the gods with their clubs.

"Spare us," screamed the gods, "We meant no harm. Turn us round and we will kick you closer to your island of Ono."

So now the island grew near, and at last the canoe grated on the sandy beach. Trees grew close to the sea, and a river of clear water sparkled in the sunshine; many smiling men and women stood on the shore to greet the voyagers.

"This is indeed a good land," said the men of Livuka. "Let us go ashore to meet these pleasant people and make our home with them."

They left the children to take care of the canoe and guard the gods while their elders danced the spear dance.,

As soon as the elders had gone, the gods begged the children to loosen their bonds. "If you untie us, we will teach you a strange and beautiful song."

The children were eager to learn a new song, all except one boy, who was alarmed and distrusted the gods.

"No, we must not untie them," he said. "Our fathers will thrash us if they find we have done this. If they had wanted the gods to be free they would have untied them before they left."

But the children took no notice of him. As soon as they were free, the gods said, "Sit down. We will climb the mast and sing our song to you." They went right to the top and sang:

> Tuvana island! Tuvana below!
> Nasali can be seen from here.
> Burotu, we two are hiding here.

Tuvana and Nasali are the names of the islets that can be seen from Ono, but Burotu has never been discovered by mortals. Sometimes it is seen when the sun shines on it, but ever as canoes approach it fades from view. Burnt out torches with unusual shell bands, used by fishermen, are occasionally washed up on the beaches of Ono. Those who find them say, "See, the torches from Burotu."

The children were delighted to hear the song of the gods, and clapped their hands; they did not notice that the gods were pressing the canoe down. Suddenly the water gushed over the sides, and the canoe sank to the bottom.

When the older people returned from their dance there was no sign of the canoe, but the bodies of their children were washing to and fro in the waves.

Now when the moon shines on the waters of the Ono passage, the voices of the children may still be heard singing the plaintive song of the gods:

> Tuvana island! Tuvana below!
> Nasali can be seen from here.
> Burotu, they two are hiding there.

The people of Livuka will never forget the evil gods who drowned their children and kicked the island of Ono so far from Lakeba. The gods' physical form remained as two upright stones on the reef at Tuvana, directly in a line with the enchanted spirit world of Burotu. For many generations the two stones were heard to chant:

"Burotu, Burotu, we two are hiding there."

FOOD AND WATER FROM MOALA

AT one time many canoes used to visit Fiji and the Lau islands from Tonga. Some were brought by storms, and if the crew was small and unarmed, the men were in danger of being killed; but if they were large canoes filled with fighting men, they would be well received, and entertained with feasts and dancing until they were ready to return.

It was such a war canoe that came once to Moala, bearing a noble chief of Tonga and a company of fighting men. Before they left, the chief of Moala gave his daughter, Roko-vaka-ola, to the visiting chief. The young woman, who was lovely and gentle, was bitterly grieved, because she had already been chosen by Kubu-ni-vanua, the great god of Moala.

She begged her father not to send her away with the Tongans.

"I shall be unhappy there, if you make me go," she said. "I shall never see you or my mother again; and who knows what will happen when Kubu-ni-vanua finds that I have gone!"

Her father was troubled.

"I would give a great deal to keep you with me," he replied. "But this chief from Tonga is a powerful man, and his fighting men outnumber ours. I dare not send him away empty-handed, now that I have promised you to him."

In spite of her tears, Roko-vaka-ola was put on board the Tongan canoe and carried away to far-distant Tungua. Her husband was kind and built a vine-house for her, but still she grieved and wept aloud when she was alone.

Kubu-ni-vanua heard the sound of his beloved weeping, and flew to her to see what troubled her.

"Why are you crying, my loved one?" he asked as he entered her house.

She rushed into his arms.

"Take me back to Moala," she begged. "I have no fault to find with my husband, but I long for you, and my own people, and for the fair land that used to be my home. Tungua is bare and unfriendly. There is little food and hardly any water on this island. My soul faints for my own land."

Kubu-ni-vanua comforted her gently: "Alas, my dear one, I cannot take you back with me. You belong now to your husband. But at least I can bring you food and water. It will make life easier for you, and will remind you that you will always be loved by the god of your own home."

He flew back to Moala, to Matamatakalou, near Cakova, and there he took one of the large leaves of the dalo. He twisted it into the shape of a cup and filled it with clear water. Dusk had turned to the starry banner of night by the time he reached Tungua and laid his offering before the woman he loved.

When Roko-vaka-ola woke the next morning she went to the door of her house with a smile on her lips, for in her dreams she had been held in the arms of the god who was her lover. Looking down expecting to see the dry ground, she was astonished to see a spring of clear water bubbling up and singing a song to comfort her as it rippled over the stone. On its bank grew many dalo plants, excellent to eat.

So Roko-vaka-ola's soul grew light. She knew that these were signs that the god had visited her again, and that while the stream flowed, giving her cool sparkling water to drink and nourishing dalo to eat, she would be sharing the gifts of her homeland with her lover.

The memory of the voyage of the god to his mortal lover will never be forgotten so long as the dalo trees of Matamatakalou flourish on the Tongan island of Tungua.

HOW THE ISLAND OF ROTUMA WAS MADE

Two hundred miles north of the main islands of Fiji, and many miles westward of Samoa, lies the tiny island group called Rotuma. These islands have not always been there. Long ago there was only empty sea, stretching on and on, almost without end.

In those days there lived in Samoa a chief named Raho who had two grandchildren; a boy called Lama, and a girl whose name was Maiva. Although the two children had the same grandfather they had different grandmothers, because Raho had married two wives.

The children were always quarrelling.

"Your grandmother was only an inferior wife!" Lama used to taunt Maiva. "You're a no-account girl, you're a foreigner!"

Maiva was unhappy when Lama called her such ugly names. He would never leave her alone, and at last she became desperate. She went to her grandfather and said, "Please, Grandfather, take me away to some other island where you and I can live together, and Lama will leave me alone."

"I know you are unhappy, Maiva," Raho said kindly. "I have told Lama to stop teasing you. But if he won't, I can't do anything to help you. You see, his grandmother was my first wife – but that doesn't stop me loving you very dearly indeed. You will always be my favourite grandchild."

"Please, *please*, grandfather," Maiva begged, "you don't want me always to be unhappy, do you? Nobody likes an unhappy girl. When I grow up no one will want to marry me if I am always miserable."

"Very well, then," Raho said. "I will give you servants to look after you, and men to paddle a canoe, and you can go away and find another island where you can live in peace with your friends."

"No, I don't want that either," wailed Maiva. "I want you with me, dear Grandfather. I could never be happy without you."

The old chief looked at her in consternation.

"But how could I possibly do that, Maiva? My chief wife would never forgive me, nor my son; nor even Lama himself. After all, he is my grandson!"

"Dear grandfather," Maiva begged again, "just think how

happy we would be together. Both your families quarrel; but I love you and you love me too."

The chief turned away without a word. All that night he lay awake, thinking about what his dear grand-daughter had said. In the morning his mind was made up. He told his best craftsmen to fell a large tree and to build a canoe. This took a long time. Raho was worried because he saw that Maiva was growing thin, and Lama seemed to be even more cruel to her. Neither he nor Maiva had told anyone about their plans, and when the canoe was ready to launch, everybody in the village came down to watch or to help. They pushed it into the water and exclaimed in admiration as it rested as lightly as a bird on the sea, with its prow raised high in the air.

The same night Raho secretly put food and water on board the canoe, and two coconut leaf baskets of soil from his island home of Savaii.

As night fell Raho boarded the canoe with a few trusted followers, and with his grand-daughter Maiva. Quietly the plaited pandanus leaf sail was raised, and as it caught the wind the canoe heeled over and sped out towards the west. Day after day and night after night the canoe went on, always heading towards the red sunset. There were many leagues of ocean behind them when Raho decide that they had gone far enough. In all their sailing they had seen no sign of land, not even the towering cumulus clouds which indicate a lonely island somewhere over the horizon.

"Throw the baskets of soil into the sea," he told his servants. Wondering at the command, they tossed the contents of the coconut-leaf baskets over the side. Instead of sinking beneath the waves the Samoan soil grew and grew, until at last it was one large island, nine miles in length, with hills and valleys and wonderful beaches, with coconut palms waving in the breeze, and luscious yellow oranges growing in groves. The canoe grounded on its sandy shore, and when the party went inland they found yams, as long as a man growing in the fertile soil. Then they looked out to sea, and noticed that a little of the soil had been spilled at some distance and had formed another island a few miles away.

Raho called the place Rotuma, and this name has remained during all the years that have followed. Rotuma is a lovely island. It still has coconut palms, oranges all the year round, and fertile garden soil for the yams, while its inhabitants are more like the Samoans than the Fijians, with language and dances resembling closely the Tongan language and the Tongan dances. Some of their customs are rather like those of people who live further away to the north, nearer the equator.

The descendants of Raho and of his grand-daughter Maiva are a happy people who owe their beautiful island home to the courage of Raho, the chief of Savaii, and to his beloved little grand-daughter Maiva.

HOW BUA GOT ITS NAME

THE first people to land on the shores of Fiji anchored their canoes and settled at Vuda on the west coast of Viti Levu. The name of the canoe was Kaunitoni. Their chief, Lutunasobasoba, whose name is greatly revered by his descendants, is regarded as the founder of the Fijian race.

He had many sons. When they became men, they quarrelled amongst themselves, and their father became so tired of their disputes that he told them he did not ever want to see them again. So they all left their home at Vuda and scattered in different directions; some went to the interior of the island, and others to the eastern coast.

One of these sons, Rokomautu, settled at Verata. After his marriage he had many sons – so many that he could not make up his mind which of them should succeed him as head of the tribe when he died.

These grandsons of Lutumasobasoba were as quarrelsome as their fathers. One of them left Verata and sailed away to find some other place in which to live, and this was a cause of sadness to his mother, because he was her favourite son. When he left, she went down to the beach to say goodbye to him. The tears ran down her face as she gave him a branch of frangipani, or bua tree, which she had broken off.

"Wherever you finally make your home, please plant this branch of bua," she said.

He kissed his mother and promised that he would do as she asked. Then, with the branch of bua in his hand, he stepped aboard his canoe where his men were already manning the sail.

"Moce!" called the people on the shore. "Goodbye."

"Moce!" answered the men on the canoe.

Lifting to the waves, it sped to the north-west, passing the northernmost part of Viti Levu, past Malake Island, until it approached Vanua Levu, where the canoe anchored and the men went ashore.

The young chief remembered his promise and planted the branch of bua. The rains came, the branch took root, put out young shoots and grew into a vigorous tree. It bore green leaves, which fell off, and were followed by rich, sweet-smelling flowers.

Year after year the tree blossomed. The young man and his followers broke off the branches and planted them, and soon there was a grove of bua trees.

"Let us call this place Bua," said the people. And so it received its name, and by that name it is known to this very day.

HOW YANUCA GOT ITS NAME

In Viti Levu, near the village of Deuba, there is a range of hills. In a village on its slopes there lived a chief who had one son, whose only interest was spearing fish on the sea shore. He was perfectly happy so long as he was left to do this all day long.

This boy had been spoilt by his father. When he was quite young he had been given a house and men servants to look after him. He never played with other children. He was guarded strictly by his servants, and was not allowed to talk to other boys and girls.

In these circumstances the young man grew up without any knowledge of young women and their ways, for he had hardly ever seen a girl in his life except at a distance.

On the other side of the range of hills there lived another chief who had an only daughter. Her father had brought her up sensibly, and she had grown into a greatly desired young woman. This girl, whose name was Raluve, had made a pet of a large crayfish which lived in a pool where she bathed every day.

At this time the young chief, whose full name was Ravouvouni-Burelotu, used to go down to the shore to spear fish each day. On one occasion he met his father who said, "When you go to the sea shore, which way do you go — to the left or to the right?"

"I always go to the left, until I find a good place to spear fish."

"I am glad to hear that," said his father. "You must always go to the left; never to the right."

"Why is that?"

"If you went to the right you would find the coast curves round the end of the range of hills where we live; I want you to promise me never to go there."

"I shall remember your words, my father," said the young man.

He had no thought of disobeying, though he wondered why his father had imposed this restriction on him. The chief had made it because he did not want Ravouvou to marry any girl except one of his own choosing, and was especially anxious that he should never meet Raluve, for her father was his bitterest enemy.

One day Ravouvou went fishing and, seeing a shoal of fish near the shore to the right, he forgot his father's advice and followed after it. The pursuit took him round the point which marked the end of the mountain range, and into the domain of Raluve's father. Presently Ravouvou came to the pool where Raluve bathed each day, and was excited to see the giant crayfish lurking at the bottom. He thrust his spear through the water, impaled it, and brought it to the surface, but it was so huge that he was unable to lift it out of the pool. It struggled to free itself from the point of the spear, which was nearly jerked out of Ravouvou's hand.

The young man jumped into the water, but when he came to the surface he was so surprised that he let the crayfish go. For there, just a few feet from him, was a young woman bathing in the pool. They looked into each other's eyes and fell in love, without a single word being spoken between them.

Even in his wildest dreams Ravouvou had never imagined that he would meet a young woman of such perfection, while she was equally attracted to the handsome young chief. She climbed out of the pool, dressed, and together they walked along the beach.

"If we are seen," she said, "we shall be both punished by death. Let us run away."

"But where could we go?" asked Ravouvou.

'Do you see that island far away on the horizon, to the west of Beqa? It is uninhabited. No one would ever dream that we would go there. Here is a canoe. If we go now we shall be out of sight before we are missed."

So the young man pushed the canoe down into the water. They raised the sail and with a favourable wind crossed quickly to the island.

"Let us call it Yacuva," Ravouvou said when they reached the shore. "We have reached the place that will be our home for ever, therefore it must be called Yacuva, which means 'reach'."

They found fruit and many kinds of fish, and they lived happily together for many years. Several children were born to them. Eventually they reached old age and died. Their children's children multiplied, until the island was fully inhabited.

The island that they named in their joy has now been altered over the years to Yanuca, but even in its changed form it commemorates the romance of Ravouvou and Raluve.

CHAPTER VI
THE MAKING OF ISLANDS

WHY MOCE IS LARGER THAN ONEATA

WHEN the world was young there were many gods, who used to fly from one part of the world to another. They had no home, but were allowed to build new islands for themselves, on one condition: the work was to be completed in a single night. This meant that if a large island was to be made, the gods had to work extremely hard to get it finished before the dawn came.

Two of these gods were flying through the air one day, and they came to Lakeba.

"I should very much like to build an island near here for myself," said one of them.

"So should I," the other repleid. "Let us go and ask the god of Lakeba for some soil."

They made this request and were given permission to take as much as they wanted from the highest hill on the island. Its name was Kedekede, which means "All of us".

As night fell the two gods flew up to the hill and filled their coconut leaf baskets as quickly as they could, each trying to finish before the other.

Ramosi was a lazy god, but for once he worked hard, hoping that he could finish his task quickly and snatch a little sleep before the dawn came. When his baskets were filled he swung the carrying-stick over his shoulder and took the soil to a place some distance from the island of Lakeba. He tipped it into the ocean and hurried back for a second load.

Tuwara was quite different. He had decided that he would build a tremendously large island, taking the whole night over it.

"I must make my reef well to the south-west," he said. "Then I shall have plenty of room for a really sizeable island."

First of all he dropped some stones to make the reef that is now called Bukatatanoa or Argo reef; then he went back to Lakeba for earth to make an island inside the reef. But presently he was startled by an unusual sound – *cockadoodledoo* – *cockadoodledoo*! It was many hours before dawn, so the cockcrow startled Tuwara. He didn't realise that the lazy Ramosi was playing a trick on him.

Ramosi had taken only three loads out to sea, but had finished making a beautiful circular island not far from Lakeba, and was quite satisfied with his work and ready for sleep. In fact he had been indulging in a short nap when he was woken up by the sound of Tuwara flying overhead with loads of soil.

"I must stop that fellow!" he said, and gave a strident cock crow that echoed round the hills.

Tuwara was upset. He was deceived by his friend's trick and, thinking that the sun would soon be rising, he decided to abandon his plan for an ambitious island. Unfortunately he had spent so much time making the Bukatatanoa reef that he had made little progress with the island itself. Now he worked hastily and clumsily. He put one of the baskets upside down and made it into a hill, which is called Kedekede after the mother hill on Lakeba. From the other basket soil fell into the sea, making a small island called Lawa.

In his haste he dropped his carrying-stick, which was turned into a reef of black stone; but still the protecting barrier round his island was not completed. He rushed backwards and forwards, gathering stones to make a reef to encircle all the islands that he had formed. Such a peculiar reef it was! It was an untidy piece of work and there were three gaps in it.

When daylight dawned Tuwara looked across the ocean and saw that Ramosi was laughing at him. He was angry, but he had to be content with his tiny, carelessly shaped island, with its peculiar reef with the three openings in it, and the great Argo reef many miles away, witnessing to his grandiose plans. There was nothing he could do about it. He called his island Oneata, which means "an upper place".

Ramosi, the cunning one, the sleepy-head, called his island Moce, which means "sleep". In spite of the little work that he did on it, Moce is larger than Oneata because of the trick that Ramosi played on his friend Tuwara.

HOW THE SANDHILLS OF NADROGA WERE MADE

A POWERFUL giant of Kadavu, who had the gift of flight, was in search of land. He had no place that he could call his own, and when in the distance he saw some hills, he thought they might suit his purpose.

He flew there, dug some of the soil with a pointed digging-stick, placed it on his back, and flew off with it over the sea, intending to place it where he could build an island on which to live.

The owner of the hills also had the power of flight. He saw the giant and gave chase. The thief flew as fast as he could, but his pursuer began to catch up with him. Some of the soil fell from his wings into the sea, and this formed the island of Beqa.

Then a storm blew up. The giant was tossed from one side to another, and little dribbles of soil fell from his back, forming the islands of Nukulau, Makuluva, Yanuca, and Vatulele.

Some of these islands became fertile gardens where coconut trees, bananas, yams, pawpaw, and dalo grow in profusion. But the thief was not permitted to enjoy them. The chase went on and on until they reached the great island of Viti Levu. The giant was tiring by this time, and all that was left of his precious load was a little sand. By this time he had outdistanced his pursuer and was able to alight at Nadroga on the south-west coast. The soil was gone. All that was left was sand, which was useless for growing vegetables. His daring theft had proved to be in vain.

What happened to the giant we do not know. But to this very day you may go to the south-west coast of Viti Levu and see the rolling, arid sandhills that were formed from the stolen sands of Kadavu.

MOLAU AND TANOVA

KADAVU is a province which consists of an island twenty-one miles in length and a cluster of smaller islands at the northeastern end. This chain of scattered islets is called Ono. The largest of them has the same name, Ono, while the tiny islands are known as Dravuni, Buliya, Vanau Kula, Qasibale, and Aukuve.

Long ago, before the small islands existed, the god Tanova lived at the eastern end of Kadavu. He was a friend of the god of Nabukelevu in the south-west, and although their homes were far apart they were close friends, often visiting each other and enjoying a talk over their yaqona drinking.

One day while they were drinking together at the mountain of Nabukelevu, Molau, the god of that place, suggested that part of the mountain should be removed and placed in the sea, so that his domain would be extended.

The idea did not appeal to his friend Tanova. He found it impossible to agree tamely to the enlarging of another god's dominions. But because he was a guest and a friend, he did not like to openly object; so he kept his counsel, and Molau thought that he had agreed.

The yaqona drinking continued. Time after time the empty polished half coconut shell cups were spun back along the mats with cries of "maca" or empty, accompanied by the formal clapping of hands. Time after time fresh root from the gardens was pounded in the mortar, placed in a great wooden bowl, mixed with water from a bamboo container, and strained through tree fibre. The cups were filled again and pretty girls proffered them on their knees, clapping their hands in a gesture of courtesy. This is the way that yaqona is still drunk in Fiji.

Tanova was careful to avoid drinking too much, but Molau, who thought that his friend had agreed to his plan, exercised no restraint, and soon began to feel sleepy. His head nodded; he leaned against the reed walls of his home and fell fast asleep.

As soon as Tanova saw that his friend was asleep he picked up two coconut leaf baskets, filled them with soil, and set out hastily for home, carrying a basket on each end of a pole which rested on his shoulder.

Molau was not really drunk, for yaqona is not an intoxicating drink. He heard his friend leaving and woke up with a start. The

He saw his friend running with the baskets on his shoulder.

first thing he saw was a big hole in his mountain. It was the crater which can still be seen in the top of Mount Nabukelevu.

He was indignant that his friend had forestalled him. Seizing his spear of sharpened wood, he ran along the hilltops of Dagai Yawa and Tavuki, over the isthmus of Vunisea, and along the hilltops of Sanima. From this vantage point he saw his friend running with the baskets over his shoulder, and he threw his spear at him.

It missed, and Tanova ran even faster. The two gigantic gods raced along the length of Kadava Island, springing from height to height. They passed Mount Noibutu with Tanova still in the lead.

He ran so fast that when he reached the end of the island he was unable to stop, and ran on into the sea. The two coconut leaf baskets broke loose from the carrying pole and shot out over the water. One of them was unbroken and formed the island of Ono across the strait from the Kadavu mainland. But the soil in the other basket broke, and scattered as it went. This basket bounced off the sea and travelled halfway to Viti Levu, where it was changed into the great rocks of Solo. The soil that broke become the tiny islets of Dravuni, Buliya, Vanuakula, Qasibale, and Aukuve.

Tanova then became the god of Ono, for he felt it would be wise to stay away from his old friend. His descendants still live on the islands, and the people of Kadavu mainland take care not to sleep when drinking with them for, like their ancestor god, they are quick to seize an opportunity and take advantage of it.

CHAPTER VII
LEGENDS OF GIANTS

FLAMING TEETH

FLAMING Teeth was a giant who lived in a cave on Rotuma, four hundred miles north of Viti Levu. His teeth were like burning coals, and with every breath he took long tongues of flame shot in and out of his mouth. When he appeared the villagers ran as fast as they could to other caves in the hillside, hoping to escape him, but his arms were so long that he was able to reach out and snatch anyone he wanted.

In those days the people of Rotuma ate their food raw because they had no fire. One day two young men who were talking together began to make plans to get fire so that they could cook food, which would then taste so much better. A bold idea came to them. They would steal the flame from the giant's teeth!

They took a bundle of dry coconut palm leaves and tiptoed into the giant's cave. Flaming Teeth was asleep. His mouth was open, and the whole cave was lit up by the light that came from his white-hot teeth.

The young men held out the coconut leaves, so that they caught alight from the flames in the giant's teeth. When they got to the door of the cave they rushed outside and down the hillside with their torches, with the giant closely in pursuit.

The young men were fleet of foot. They managed to reach their own cave, and rolled a stone against the doorway. Flaming Teeth beat against it in vain. The young men were a little frightened as the rock trembled and shook, but they knew that it would hold up against the giant, no matter what he did.

After a while Flaming Teeth realised this and thought he would defeat them by cunning.

"Open the door," he pleaded. "Please open the door and I will sing to you."

The young men laughed at the thought of the giant singing to them, but they rolled the stone just a little to one side. Flaming Teeth tried to push his head in, but the gap was too narrow and he could not shift the stone.

He tried again.

"Young men, please open your door a little wider. I could then get my head right inside, and you could hear me sing. Don't you want to hear my song?"

The two young men rolled the stone a little further aside and the giant was able to put his head right inside the cave. The moment he did so they both caught the stone in their hands and pushed it against the far wall of the opening, crushing the giant's head.

They shouted so loudly that the villagers came running up the hill to see what was happening.

"Look at him!" the young men shouted. "Flaming Teeth is dead! We killed him, and we have stolen his fire!"

It was true. Now that the giant was dead the people had something that they had never enjoyed before – fire. They never let it go out. All night long the embers were kept smouldering after the day's cooking was finished, and first thing in the morning someone would pick up a dry coconut leaf and light it at the embers. Then large sticks were put on top, and before long a crackling fire on the earthen floor of a hut would be ready to cook delicious meals of dalo, and yam, and fish done in coconut cream.

THE GIANT AND HIS SWING

IN a tiny village in Naceva, far away in the mountains of the island of Kadavu, lived the family of Bulai. They were ordinary, hard-working people, but Bulai, the youngest member of the family was a giant who had left home at an early age to live on the tops of the mountains.

Bulai was much fonder of play than work. He made an enormous swing for himself from strong forest vines. They hung from the trees, and Bulai sat on a seat at the end of a long creeper that hung from the biggest tree in the mountains.

With one gigantic swing he could fly across the mountains and valleys for twenty miles until he came to Nabukelevu; back would go the swing, right across the island, until he was far over the sea at the other end of Kadavu.

All day long the swing went backwards and forwards, and in its passage Bulai swung right over his own village. Every time he swung past he could see his father and the women of the family at work. At one time they were climbing up a track in the forest to the yam gardens; the next time digging yams with sharp pointed sticks. Another time they would be climbing the coconut trees and cutting big leaves, while others sat on the ground plaiting the leaves into baskets.

Another swing and Bulai saw them putting the yams into the basket, taking strong poles which they placed over their shoulders, and carrying the heavy baskets home. Back went the swing again, and he could see them slipping and sliding in the mud up and down the hills, back to their own village.

As the swing went by in the evening he could see the women gathering firewood and carrying it to their home and, when it was almost too dark to see, the first flickering of the fires that were lit to roast the yams.

·At that moment Bulai would stretch out his hand and snatch the roasted yams away from his family just as they were ready to eat them.

They were good-natured people, and at first, although they grumbled about it, they just went out and got more yams. But as day after day went by and Bulai snatched all their food as his swing hurtled over the village, they knew that something would have to be done about it. They shouted at him, but Bulai just laughed and took no notice.

One day two men went out of the village carrying stone axes. They climbed far up the hills until they came to the top, to the tree from which the giant swing was hanging. Up the tree they went until they could see right across the island and far out to sea. Below them was the creeper that Bulai used for a swing. They chopped at it until it parted; as it fell it coiled up in the valley far below like a snake, with Bulai entangled in it. He was killed instantly.

In a village somewhere in Naceva there are two large white stones which look like the bones of a giant. The people call them Bulai's Bones, and every time they look at them they say: "Those who think only of pleasure and leave all the work to others will come to a bad end!"

THE GIANT WHO WENT TO LOOK FOR WATER

RATUVA, the giant who lived in Namara in Kadavu,was proud of his home. The villagers had built it for him of tree trunks and reeds and leaves. The women wove floor mats of pandanus leaves for Ratuva to lie on. They planted yams and dalo in his garden as food for him to eat, and every day the men went out to the reef and brought home shellfish. The more adventurous ones made big outrigger canoes, and sailed out to the deep sea beyond the reef to catch other fish. Fishing nets were made of string from the bark of trees, and the women took them into the sea and brought back hundreds of red, white, blue, yellow, and black fish, all wriggling and struggling to get out of the net. These they cooked for Ratuva.

The bark of trees was beaten into cloth for him to wear, and he was rightly proud of everything that was done for him.

When he called out sternly, "Come here," the people came running to see what he wanted. If he said, "Fan me," they fanned him. If he wanted them to sit still and be quiet, they sat still and were quiet. If he wanted them to sing to him, they sang their ancient songs. If he wanted to drink yaqona, the roots were brought into his house, the prettiest girls chewed it and spat it out into a big wooden bowl, mixed it with water, and offered it to Ratuva in a half coconut shell.

There was only one thing that troubled the giant: there was no fresh water anywhere to be found in Namara. He was sorry for his people because when they needed fresh water they had to take long sections of bamboo, as thick as a man's arm, and walk for many miles through the forest to the home of another giant to ask him for water.

This was a continual hurt to Ratuva's pride, so at length he decided to bring water to his home to save his people from having to work so hard.

By his magic powers he flew to Mamalata, where there was a beautiful pool of clear water. When he arrived at the pool he picked a large dalo leaf and dipped it in the pool. He held it up by the corners and lifted it up full of water. The leaf was so large that when he had finished there was no water left in the pool.

He had nearly reached his home at Namara when the dalo

leaf split, and the water was spilt. Fortunately it fell into a big mangrove tree, and the water trickled down into a fork between two large branches.

Since that day the people of Namara are able to get fresh water whenever they want it from the fork of a big mangrove tree which is still to be found in a swamp near the sea-shore.

KUMAKU AND THE GIANT

KUMAKU was a healthy, happy little girl with sturdy limbs and an active body, with bright black eyes dancing with fun and shining with happiness. Her straight black hair hung down to her shoulders, and often she'd place a flower above one ear. Like many other small girls she was sometimes as naughty as she was beautiful.

One day when her mother was cooking food for dinner she called to Kumaku.

"Kumaku," she said, "take this coconut shell and bring me some water."

Kumaku took the shell and said, "Do you want fresh water from the spring?"

"Oh no," said her mother, "I want sea water please; then I won't need to put any salt in it, and I have been too busy lately to make salt."

As Kumaku ran down the path her mother called after her, "Keep away from the spiders' webs!"

Kumaku knew what she meant. There were giants on the island of Rotuma. Their presence was always indicated by spiders' webs, which were strung across the path. Unwary travellers were caught in them and captured by the giants and eaten. Kumaku thought she knew better than her mother, as little girls often do, so when she came to a path that led through the bush, and saw the spiders' webs across it, she ran down it, singing a song which she knew the giants would hear. This is the song:

> Kumaku
> Draws water from the sea,
> Come with me, giants,
> Come and help me.

Before she had finished the song two giants sprang out of the bushes, picked her up and carried her down to the sea, where she filled the coconut shell with water.

The giants towered over her, but Kumaku gave a little smile, and as they reached out their hands with their long claws, she sang again:

> Blow, winds from Fiji,
> Blow up the black sand of the sea,
> Fill the giants' eyes
> So that they cannot see.
>
> Blow, winds from Tonga,
> Blow up the white sea sand,
> Dazzle their eyes
> While I fly to the land.

These were magic words, because they were part of a magic song. Immediately a strong wind blew in from the sea, carrying with it black sand and white sand hundreds of miles across the ocean, from Fiji and from Tonga. It blew into the giants' eyes so that they were blinded and could not see. They groped for her, but she easily dodged them, ran up the path, and gave the coconut shell full of salt water to her mother just as though nothing had happened.

RAVOUVOU THE DART THROWER

A POPULAR game in Fiji is called veitiqa, or dart throwing. The darts, or tiqa, are polished, egg-shaped pieces of wood, pointed at one end, and several inches in length. A long reed is placed firmly in a slot at the blunt end of the dart, and used to hurl it through the air.

Long ago there was an ancient god of Kadevu whose name was Ravouvou. One day he woke from sleep in the cool of a late afternoon and thought he would like to play at veitiqa for a while. But when he tried to place the reed in his ulutoa, as the egg-shaped head is called, he found that it would not fit firmly in the hole. It needed some bark cloth, which is called masi or tapa, to keep it firm. He searched everywhere but was unable to find any cloth. So, thinking that an old fishing net might serve his purpose, he sent one of his servants to the god of fishermen to ask for an old fishing net.

The god of fishermen gladly supplied him with a piece of old net, and Ravouvou was able to make the reed firm in the socket. He stood on a mountain far inland, in the Maceva district, and whirled the dart round his head. Then he took a step backwards in order to put all his weight into the throw. Five miles backwards he went, so that one foot remained at Levulevukana, while the other one was at Verata.

With a piercing, whistling sound the dart hurtled through the air, coming to rest twenty miles away at Nakasaleka.

The dart was a magic one, as befitted a god. When it came to earth it slid along the ground, crossed three valleys, and continued its swift journey right over to the Yasawa Islands, where it floated in the sea.

The god-giant put his hand up to his eyes to find where his dart had landed. It was so large that he could see it bobbing up and down on the waves. But the effort had been so tremendous that he was overcome by giddiness, and for two whole days he was unable to shake off this feeling and he staggered wherever he went.

He thought the only way that he could put an end to the giddiness was to drink some hot soup. He asked the god of fishermen if he could provide him with some and, as soon as it was heated, a big bowl was given to him. He drank it at a draught and felt better at once.

Grateful for the help of the fishermen's god, he promised that in future he would get his servants to provide the god with all the firewood he needed.

"I will flood the mountain rivers," he said. "They will bring you down all the wood you need for your fires."

Ravouvou kept his promise. In the rainy season the flood waters tumbled down the mountainside, carrying with them masses of firewood, which piled up on the beaches at the mouths of the rivers.

"If there is not enough, do not be afraid to ask for more," Ravouvou assured his friend the fisherman god, "but I don't think that you will ever need to ask, because I will supply you with all you need. Whenever you have enough, just blow a conch-shell and I'll command the floods to subside."

To this day, in the village of Joma a conch shell is blown when the floods subside, because the people of that village have never forgotten the promise that the forest god made to the fishermen's god.

SUNA, WHO WAS GREEDY

SUNA, a giant who lived in the district of Ba, on the north-west coast of Viti Levu, had an enormous appetite which could never be satisfied. The people brought him yams a yard long, and bunch after bunch of bananas. When he had eaten all that they brought, Suna would call out, "More, more, more!" till the people were wearied to death.

On one occasion an invitation was brought to the people of Ba to attend the feast at Bua on the island of Vanua Levu.

Suna was not in the village when the invitation came.

"What luck!" the people said. "Suna knows nothing about this invitation. We will not tell him!"

Their mouths were already watering at the thought of the feast – of fish cooked in coconut cream, of crab flesh baked in the embers of the fire, of dalo cooked on hot stoves, of roasted yam and ripe bananas, and juicy yellow pawpaws and golden oranges.

They made their preparations as quickly as they could, hoping that they would be completed before Suna returned.

There was much to do. They rubbed oil over their bodies to make them glisten; the best tapa clothing was chosen so that they would look gay and festive at the feast; sleeping mats and little wooden pillows were put into the canoes, and presents for the Bua people, especially brown salt made from sea water, packed into hard solid masses in the brown fibre baskets. It was a luxury they knew that the people of Bua would enjoy.

Singing ancient chants to express their happiness, they began the long crossing between Viti Levu and Vanua Levu.

When Suna returned to the village he was surprised to find it was nearly empty. There were a few old women who were not fit to travel, and one old man.

"Where are all the people?" asked Suna.

When the old man told him what had happened the giant was very angry. He made a float or raft of light wood and using this to support him, he swam after the canoes. So big was he, and so strong, that before long he passed the canoes, but at such a distance that the people in them did not see him.

He reached the village of Bua long before the canoes came in sight, and waded ashore. He found that the people of Bua had

The party was over; all the food was eaten.

yams stacked in piles many feet in height, and had made hundreds of bunches of bananas ready for the visitors. The villagers were surprised to see Suna walking up the beach, and even more surprised that he had swum from his home instead of coming by canoe, but they were too polite to ask him why he had done so strange a thing. They welcomed him kindly and took him to a house to rest.

"Would you like some food?"

"Yes, please, I would,"

They brought him cooked yams, which he quickly gobbled up.

"Could I have some more please?"

They brought a much larger helping, but he gulped it down as greedily as the first supply.

"Could I have some more, please?"

They went away and whispered to each other.

"He may be a giant, but what a terrible appetite he has!" They called for more helpers, and presently men came staggering in with scores of bunches of bananas, and piles upon piles of yams. Suna ate up every one of them. More yams were brought; more dalo were carried in; and still Suna was hungry.

"More, more!" he cried, licking his lips.

Long before the canoes arrived from Ba, Suna had eaten up every crumb of food in the village. But the Bua people, noted for their politeness, entertained him with dances; women sat on the floor mats singing their old chants, and girls with garlands of flowers waved their hands in graceful action songs.

In the late afternoon the Ba canoes grated on the beach, and the hungry voyagers leaped ashore. There was no one to welcome them!

"What can all that singing be?" they asked one another. "How strange it is for our friends to be singing before we have arrived!"

As there was no one about, some of the young men ran up to the village. They quickly realised what had happened. The party was over; all the food was eaten. There was nothing for them to do but to sail back to Ba, hungry, tired, and disappointed.

To this very day if anyone is too greedy they say, "He is just like Suna!"

CHAPTER VIII

MONSTERS AND SUPERNATURAL CREATURES

THE MONSTER OF CAKAUDROVE

A NUMBER of villagers from the coast of Cakaudrove had spent a long day at sea, fishing. It had been a hot and tiring day, and they were wearied with their labours. They were still a long way from shore, and when one of them suggested spending the night on a small island and returning to the mainland the next morning, the others gladly agreed.

There was a full moon that night, and the beach shone like silver, except where the exhausted fishermen lay in the black shadows of the trees. Suddenly they were awakened by a prolonged scream. They started up to their feet and looked at each other in terror. Someone shouted, "A monster! Look!"

They saw a huge, lizard-like creature, its scales winking in the moonlight, rear up and up until it towered above the trees. With horror they saw the legs of a man dangling from its fanged mouth. The monster lowered itself to the ground, slithered across the sand, and plunged into the sea. The water foamed round the repulsive body as it disappeared slowly beneath the waves.

For a moment they were speechless and immobile. Then, as one man, they turned and rushed in panic to the shelter of the bush.

Only one of their number remained: a boy, who had slept soundly through all the disturbance. In the morning he was surprised to find that the men were no longer there, but a swift glance assured him that their canoe was still on the beach. Thinking they had gone into the bush to find food, he ran across the sand and plunged into the sea for his daily swim.

The rest of the crew were returning to the place where their sleep had been so frightfully disturbed, when they heard another high-pitched scream. They broke through the screen of bushes in time to see the gigantic lizard's teeth crunching through the boy's body. Then the monster sank out of sight.

Some of them lined the beach, while others paddled backwards and forwards, peering down into the clear water, their spears beside them ready to be thrust into the creature that had killed two of their party. They spent the morning anxiously searching and waiting, but saw no sign of the monster, and came to the conclusion that its hunger was satisfied and that it had gone away.

Before nightfall they had sailed back to their own village on

She was absorbed in her task.

MONSTERS AND SUPERNATURAL CREATURES

the mainland. As it grew dark they gathered round in the grass houses and discussed the matter at length over the yaqona bowls. Many were the speculations that were made that night, and it was agreed that the visitation had been made by a god in the form of a monster, to punish them for some crime or breach of tabu of which they had been unaware.

Both men and women went about their everyday tasks quietly, as a malignant, brooding silence fell over the village. In the late afternoon one of the women was busy washing dalo roots in a saltwater lagoon at some distance from the beach. She was absorbed in her task and did not notice a huge shape gliding through the rushes that lined the edge of the lagoon. The long neck extended, the lizard's mouth opened wide, and the woman was swallowed whole. A small boy gave the alarm, and the men snatched up their spears and formed a long line to block the monster from the sea.

The lizard blinked its eyes and turned its head slowly from side to side. Seeing there was no way of escaping the spears it lumbered forward, crushing the reeds and leaving a slimy trail into which the water seeped and gurgled. Soon it was standing on the sandy beach and the spears were rattling against its scales like hailstones and bouncing off harmlessly.

Day after day the sea lizard returned and claimed another victim, until nearly a dozen people had lost their lives. The beach and the lagoon were deserted, and the villagers stayed huddled in their houses, not daring to venture out lest they should be seen by the monster.

"This is intolerable!" said an old man. "Why should grown men and women have to spend their lives like crabs huddled in their holes?"

"But what can we do, old man? No spear can pierce its hide. No knife can penetrate its scales. We are lost. We are dead. We are as good as buried in the belly of the monster."

"We are still men, and we can act like men. The gods have given us fingers on our hands and brains in our skulls. They expect us to use them, instead of putting our heads in our hands like frightened children. Listen to me."

They drew closer and listened to the plan he put before them. Their eyes brightened and sleep was sounder that night than it had been for a long while.

The old man had observed the spot where the monster emerged from the sea each time it came ashore. The path to the village led from this point past a large vesi tree. On the old man's instructions a rope was passed over a stout branch and hung in a wide noose which was concealed by the undergrowth. Many strong men hid in the bushes holding on to the end of the rope, and waited to hear the shout that would tell them to tighten it.

When these preparations were complete, the old man sauntered along the beach, looking constantly at the water from under his bushy eyebrows. Presently the waters swirled and the long, hideous snout of the monster broke from the waves. The old man turned and ran along the path that led to the village. He had a good start, but he had not reckoned on the speed with which the lizard could move on dry land. Once he stumbled over a root and fell headlong. He could hear the monster breathing close behind him, but he scrambled to his feet again and raced onwards.

The ground shook under the tread of the four-footed monster, which was gaining on him quickly. At last the vesi tree came in sight. He sprang through the noose, gave a feeble cry, and collapsed on the path.

As the monster pounced, the noose was drawn tight. The rope tightened round its neck and foreleg; though it thrashed and struggled till the tree swayed and groaned with the strain, it could not break free. Carefully avoiding the flailing legs and tail, the men watched their chance and worked sharp spear points between the scales, hammering the heads and shafts home through the tough hide and belabouring it with clubs.

At long last the monster quivered and lay dead. The women and children and the old men and old women came out to see it. With great labour they hacked off its limbs and roasted them on the fire.

Many satisfied people lay down to sleep that night, after singing the praises of the brave old man who had saved them from the ghastly sea-lizard; but there were still one or two who whispered to each other in dark corners, and said that evil would come to the village because Samulayo, the Killer of Souls, must surely have sent his servant from the unearthly village of Nabagatai to compass their death.

THE PHANTOM CANOE

THE young chief Raluve and his grandmother lived all alone on the island of Burotokula. Although he was greatly loved by his grandmother it was a lonely life for a young man.

Sometimes young women came over from other islands by canoe, but the ever-vigilant grandmother made sure that no girl was ever left alone with Raluve.

Occasionally Raluve complained so much that he and his grandmother paid a visit to other islands; but while they were away from home the grandmother was as watchful of him as ever.

It was but natural that such a handsome and closely guarded young man should become attractive to girls, and he had many admirers. Some who were of noble birth sent servants to him with gifts, and it is said that every day canoes arrived at Burotokula, piled high with coconuts, yams, woven mats, tapa cloth, shells and turtles. Sometimes the servant brought whale's teeth and presented them ceremonially, with a request that Raluve should marry the sender.

The young man himself was not tempted by these gifts; he always gave a whale's tooth to the servant and asked to be excused.

One day while he was bathing in a pool of fresh water near his home, he was startled by a loud cry. The sound seemed to come from his own house. He ran there as quickly as he could, and was horrified to see that two witches were clutching his grandmother by the throat. In a few moments she would have been strangled.

As soon as Raluve appeared they dropped the old lady, slipped through the door, and scuffled quickly away, with Raluve in hot pursuit. They sped along the reef with Raluve following, but unfortunately he did not notice that a great clam shell or vasua was lying there, and he put his foot right inside it. The valves clamped shut, and the young chief was caught firmly by the foot. The witches disappeared in the distance and he was left alone on the reef with his foot caught firmly in the giant clam, knowing that before long the tide would rise and he would be drowned.

It was fortunate for the young man that at this time a lovely young chieftainess from a nearby island happened to be travelling in her canoe in search of shellfish from the reef. Seeing his plight she went to his rescue, and managed to release him.

It was a happy day for both Raluve and the young woman who had come to his rescue. It was a terrible danger that had brought them together, but it was love that bound them closer to one another.

Supported by the girl, the young man hobbled ashore and managed to persuade his old grandmother, who had now recovered from the witches' attack, that it would be a good thing if they were to get married.

The wedding was held on the island where the bride lived, and Raluve was accompanied by his grandmother. Feasts and dancing and songs continued until late in the night. But when the celebrations were over, Raluve and his wife said farewell and prepared to leave for their own island home. The bride's relatives invited the grandmother to stay with them a little longer as their guest, and with difficulty she was persuaded to stay.

It may well be that it was a lucky decision for the old woman!

The morning sun shone and the sea sparkled as everyone crowded down to the beach to see the happy couple aboard their canoe. When the last farewells were said, the little craft sped across the lagoon, and the cries of "Moce", or goodbye followed it as the wind filled the three-cornered sail, and it glided through the gap in the reef.

The canoe did not reach the island. It was never seen again. Raluve and his bride disappeared, and the canoe became a phantom ship, which is never seen by day, but at night still sails amongst the islands and coral reefs of Fiji.

THE SKIRT OF INTESTINES

EVERYONE was frightened of the old woman who lived on the island of Moala. And no wonder, for her principal food was human flesh. After she had killed a man, a woman, or a child, she ate their bodies and used their intestines to make a skirt. For this reason she was called Likuwawa, or Intestine Skirt.

Her appetite was so insatiable that all the inhabitants of the island were eaten except one old woman and her little granddaughter, Veverua. The grandmother kept the child well away from the cannibal witch, but Veverua was an inquisitive little girl. She liked to know everything that was going on, and to see everything. Over and over again she begged her grandmother, "Please Grandmother, take me to see Likuwawa – I want to see her."

Even though she knew she was being madly foolish, the old lady gave in. One morning she went with the little girl to the place where Likuwawa lived. The girl was greatly excited at the prospect of seeing the witch but the old woman went reluctantly, her heart full of fear.

When they reached the house they found that Likuwawa was out working in the plantation. As soon as she saw them she straightened herself and called out, "Good morning, my dears, welcome to my home. Let us go into the house out of the hot sunshine, and I'll see if I can find you something to eat."

But to herself she said, "Two more humans to eat!"

The little girl and her grandmother sat in the house, resting after their long walk. After a while they heard a song being chanted. In the kitchen outside the house old Likuwawa was singing:

> Dig, dig, dig the dalo,
> Chew, chew, chew the dalo,
> Chew, chew, chew Veverua,
> Chew, chew, chew grandmother,
> Dig, dig, dig the dalo.

Veverua and her grandmother looked at each other. They realised how foolish they had been, because the old woman was evidently stoking the fires ready to roast their bodies. They jumped to their feet and ran out of the house and along the path.

Fortunately Likuwawa was so busy with her chanting that time slipped by unnoticed, and when she looked in the house and saw that the guests were gone, many hours had passed by.

The grandmother could not run very quickly. Every now and then she and Veverua had to sit down to rest. While they were seated beside the path a god, who saw they were in distress, appeared before them. He asked what their trouble was, and they told him they would soon be pursued by Likuwawa.

"Hurry along and go to your own village. I will look after her when she comes," said the god.

Presently Likuwawa came in sight. She was not frightened by any god, no matter how strong and tall he might be, and a great struggle began. The god and the old woman grappled with each other, sometimes on the land, sometimes in the sea, but in the end the god triumphed, and Likuwawa, or old Intestines Skirt, was dead.

A very happy ending came of the adventure, because eventually Veverua grew into a lovely young woman, and was taken to wife by the god who had saved her from Likuwawa.

THE FRIENDLY GNOMES OF THE FOREST

AT Vuniwaivutuka, near the Navua River, there are hollow kauri and kabea trees which are inhabited by quaint little spirit creatures called Veli. They are like the gnomes of European folklore, with white skins, tiny bodies, and big heads. They have thick woolly hair, tied back in pig-tails, and wear tapa cloth garments, but this is beaten much more finely that the cloth made by any human beings. The men have several wives, who keep the tree-houses clean and tidy, cook food for their husbands, and do most of the work.

The men and women who live at Vuniwaivutuka are fond of the Veli and have only one complaint to make – that they steal iron for their tools. Apart from this regrettable habit they are welcome in the villages, where they make occasional appearances and sing sweetly to their hosts.

The fruits of the tankua and boia provide them with food, which they describe as their coconuts and plantains. Any Fijian who is incautious or foolish enough to cut down one of these plants will be jumped on by the Veli and beaten soundly for spoiling their food supplies.

As a beverage they drink yaqona. It is not the true kava of the Fiji, but is made from the wild pepper, and is called yaqoyaqona.

These are the friendliest gnomes of the forest who have come from the spirit world to live at peace with men and women, and to guard their forest houses from destruction.

CHAPTER IX
LEGENDS OF SNAKES

THE SNAKE CHIEF

THE reigning chief of Rewa banished his daughter to a remote village hidden in the hills. He was vexed with her because, instead of presenting him with a grandson, she had given birth to a snake.

The mother lived with her son for a long time, until he became a fully grown snake. She longed to be with her friends again, but there seemed to be no hope of her father relenting and allowing her to come back.

The snake could not understand this. He said to his mother one day, "You say that I cannot see my grandfather, who is the great chief. My heart is sad, because there are things that I want to talk to him about. Will you please send a message to him to say that if he will not come to us, I would like him to send his chief adviser to us?"

His mother did not think that there would be any answer, but her son persisted so much that she sent a messenger. To her surprise the chief sent his principal adviser to her son, and they began to talk together.

"The time has come for me to get married," said the snake. "Please find a wife for me and arrange a marriage."

The Mata-ni-Vanua regarded him thoughtfully from his head to the tip of his tail.

"It will not be easy to find a wife for you, I am afraid. But I will do my best."

So the Mata-ni-Vanua went on a journey. He took with him six whale's teeth, and boarded the canoe that had brought him to the village. The canoe glided down the river and crossed the lagoon to the island of Bau, where there lived a powerful chief who had two beautiful daughters.

The Mata-ni-Vanua took the six polished teeth which hung from a piece of plaited sinnet, and sat on the mats which had been spread on the floor of the chief's house.

"Will you please accept these teeth as a tribute to our friendship?" he asked.

The chief was wary. He knew that if he accepted the teeth he must grant whatever request was made. He too, had heard all about the peculiar snake-chief of Rewa. He told his own Mata-ni-

Vanua to present a whale's tooth to the ambassador, but to excuse him from accepting the six teeth from Rewa.

The ambassador left the chief's house, knowing that he would not be successful in his quest. He stayed for some time in Bau, and one day he saw a beautiful girl who was being cared for by her grandmother. On the spur of the moment he said, "Will you marry my Snake Chief?"

"Yes," said the girl. "I will marry the Snake Chief."

It was a wonderful wedding. Women plaited mats, others printed brown patterns on white tapa cloth, using banana leaves for stencils, and a great feast was made. Long lines of men with purple leaf streamers and red ginger-flower girdles, with their bodies oiled, and black soot smeared on their faces, danced the war dances of their tribes.

The only one who did not feel entirely happy was the poor girl, who found that the snake chief was cold to touch!

It was a difficult life for the brave girl, but she looked after her husband well. In spite of his appearance, he was kind and thoughtful, and she grew to love him, not for the way he looked, but for what he really was in his heart.

One day her husband said to her, "Let us go and bathe at Naililili."

She walked down to the river with her snake husband slithering through the grass close to her feet.

"Stay here," he said, when they reached the bank. "I want to bathe alone."

The young wife sat on the bank and watched her husband disappear under water. She waited a long time, but he did not return. The tears rolled down her cheeks. She knew she loved him so much that life would be empty if he did not come back.

"Oh! If only he had taken me with him!" she exclaimed.

Just then she heard a noise behind her, and when she turned round she saw a handsome young chief standing there.

"Oh! Have you seen my dear husband anywhere?" she cried. "I am afraid he is drowned."

"Dry your tears," said the man. "I am your husband."

He took her hands in his. "Listen. Before I was born I was changed into a snake by an evil spirit. It was not my fault, or my mother's, that I was compelled to be a snake for so many years. It is your loving care that has made me into a man, by the power of the Spirit-that-changes-people."

It was a happy couple that returned to the village to tell the good news to their friends. No one went to bed that night, and the next day another wedding feast was held, because all the villagers were so pleased that the marriage had proved successful.

THE GIGANTIC SNAKE

Ratu, whose full name was Ratu Nautolelevu, lived with his wife in Kadavu. They were working away together in the yam garden, which was about a mile away from the village, clearing weeds, digging with a pointed stick, and tying yam vines to poles. It was hard work, and after a while Ratu said to his wife. "I am thirsty. I am going to take this earthen jar to get water from the well."

"Good," she replied. "While you are doing that I shall finish putting the poles in the ground."

When he reached the well, Ratu was disappointed. There was no water in it, only thick mud. He looked down and saw a snake about five feet in length, coiled up in the mud. Thinking that even a snake was better than no water, he caught it firmly behind the head and took it back to his home where he put it in the biggest earthenware jar in the house.

Day after day the snake kept on growing. Soon it was too big for the jar, and had to be put into a larger one. Still the snake went on growing, and after many days Ratu realised that there was not a jar in the whole village big enough to hold his snake. It seemed to be quite tame and harmless, so they gave up trying to keep it in a jar and let it roam round the house. The strange thing that Ratu and his wife noticed was that the snake never seemed to need food.

Shortly after this, Rata's wife gave birth to a baby boy. He was their second child, for they already had a little girl whose name was Ramatau. The new baby was called Raivaele. As he grew older and began to crawl about, the snake played happily with both the children.

Then came the terrible day when the snake spoke for the first time.

"I have lived with you for a long time now, Ratu," hissed the snake, "but you have never given me any food. Did you think that I could live on air all this time? I am very hungry now. You must give me Ramatau, and I shall eat her."

The poor man was nearly distraught, but the snake was so strong and terrible, and raised its head so threateningly, that Ratu and his wife had no choice but to give their little daughter to him

Out of its body came Ramatau and Rivaele, alive and well.

to eat. They had begun to regard the snake as a god or a devil, and were frightened to anger him further.

This gruesome meal satisfied the snake for a while, but a few weeks later it was hungry again, and this time it demanded Raivaele.

With both their children sacrificed to the snake-devil, the villager and his wife were broken-hearted. They left their home and took refuge in another village. When they got there, the people of that village were eating clams, and they gave some to the two fugitives. The food strengthened them, and they were just beginning to feel reconciled to their fate when they looked up and saw the snake coming down the path towards the village. It was bigger than ever now. Its body was as large as a coconut tree trunk, and its head towered above the forest trees.

The villagers were speechless. They did not know where to run for safety.

"Give me some clam meat," the snake demanded.

When its hunger was satisfied it lay down to sleep, and the wise men gathered together to work out some plan that would rid them of the terrible creature that had come to their village. Soon their minds were made up. They went to the snake as soon as it woke up, and said,

"We are in difficulty. We wonder if you can help us?"

"What do you want me to do?"

"It is like this," said the headman of the village. "While we were gathering clams just now to provide you with a meal, we found a big one, deep under the water, too big for us to lift. It would make a wonderful feed for you, if you would get it out of the water for us."

The snake was pleased at their concern for his appetite, and accompanied the men to the reef. The tide was low, and they showed him where the clam was. The snake wriggled through the water and tried to get his head under the clam shell to lift it up. While he was struggling with it, one of the chiefs struck him a blow behind his head and killed him.

The jubilant villagers were beginning to cut it up when out of its body walked Ramatau and Rivaele, alive and well!

CHAPTER X
LEGENDS OF FISH

THE PRAWNS OF VATULELE

FROM the larger islands of Viti Levu and Vanua Levu, and from a hundred smaller islands, eager suitors hurried to Vatulele to pay court to Yalewa-ni-cagi-bula, the daughter of the chief. She was beautiful in face and form, but her heart was as hard as the stones that lined the path to her father's house. In the darkness men would stub their toes on these stones; and in the light of day far-travelled sons of famous chiefs had bruised themselves against the cold, hard heart of Yalewa.

"Will you never choose a husband from these noble suitors who come to you?" asked her father.

She tossed her head, and the black cascade of her hair swirled round her face.

"They are all so stupid," she tittered. "Canoe after canoe comes to our little island bearing silly young men with silly blank faces. They all say the same silly things and all bring the same silly gifts. I would rather be married to a banana tree than to any one of them."

"They are all in earnest and they all love you. Surely there is one among them who could make you happy?"

"Not unless he showed himself as a god among men," Yalewa cried. "I will never marry a man who comes to this island in a canoe."

"How do you expect him to come? It is too far to swim – and I fancy there are few who can fly through the air like a seagull," her father said ironically.

Yalewa's eyes sparkled.

"That is a good thought, Father," she said. "The first suitor who flies here through the air I promise to marry."

Her father was exasperated. "You talk about silly men with empty faces, but you are a silly feather-brained girl with a heart as cold as a stone at the bottom of the sea. I shall make you marry the one I choose."

The girl's eyes filled with tears.

"Oh please, Father, I was only joking. But don't you understand that I get so tired of empty speeches and full baskets of Kumara and dalo? I want someone who is bold and daring and imaginative, who will seize me in his arms and carry me away, as if – as if – well, you said it, Father, as though he were a bird."

The chief smiled.

"I still think you are a silly girl," he said, "but perhaps I understand more than you think. Let us wait a little while longer to see if this paragon of a man will come to claim you. Now I am going to the other side of the island to see whether my men have been looking after the dalo plantations properly."

As soon as he had walked round a bend in the path and was lost to sight in the trees, Yalewa wiped the tears from her eyes and began to laugh quietly to herself.

"Why should I marry anyone when it is so much better to play with my friends?" she said aloud. "Father is just as stupid as all other men. He'll be annoyed when he comes back to find that I've probably refused another man in his absence, but I'll soon get my own way. I only hope no one finds a way to the island without a canoe. Then there'll be trouble!" and she laughed until the tears began to roll down her cheeks again.

Little did she know that at that very moment a chief of noble birth and great power had determined to subdue her. He was in too much of a hurry to make the slow journey by canoe so he rolled huge stones down the mountains of his island home until they covered the beach. Throwing off his garments, he lifted the rocks one by one and tossed them into the sea. The first ones were at a little distance from the shore, but as the line of rocks began to stretch out towards Vatulele, he threw them with all his strength. They began to stretch out into the distance, until finally they lay like a string of stepping stones from the mainland to Vatulele.

He was so anxious to meet the girl whose beauty and renown had been spoken of so highly that he had no time to prepare food and valuable gifts. He snatched up a basket of cooked prawns and leaped from rock to rock until he came to the distant island.

"Where is Yalewa-ni-cagi-bula?" he asked the first person he met, and was directed to her father's home. He burst through the door and looked at the young woman, who was staring round in surprise at the sudden invasion.

"Here is Yalewa," one of her attendants said with an embarrassed laugh, indicating the chief's daughter.

The chief strode up to her.

"You are beautiful," he said. "More beautiful than ever I dreamed. I have come to take you to my home. I want you to be my wife."

Yalewa tossed her head haughtily.

"What makes you think I would consent to be your wife?" she asked. "Only today I told my father that I would never marry a man who came here by canoe."

"In what way did you want me to come?"

She considered.

"Did you fly through the air?"

He looked at her with an amused smile.

"No, my charming little lady, I didn't fly through the air. Is there any other way you would like me to come have?"

"I might consider you for a husband if you had walked across the water from the mainland."

The young man burst into a peal of laughter.

"Come with me," he said. He took her hand and led her outside. "Look! Do you see that long line of rocks? I put them there. I walked here on them. Now will you marry me?"

She glanced at his basket.

"What did you bring me as a wedding gift?"

For the first time he lost his self-assurance.

"I was in such a hurry to come to you that I had no time to bring presents, Yalewa," he stammered. "I brought you myself across the stepping-stones of the sea – and this basket of cooked prawns."

Yalewa pulled herself free. She snatched the basket out of his hand and banged him with it until it burst apart and the prawns flew far and wide. Some of them fell into a pool beside the path, where they came to life again. They are still to be found there, darting among the stones, gleaming redly in the sunshine. The inhabitants of Vatulele regard them as sacred and say that if anyone catches them and takes them away, he will never reach the mainland because his canoe will be wrecked.

Fortunately the young suitor was not dependent on a canoe. He was now so frightened of Yalewa that he ran back to his home and as he stepped on the stones they sank down to the bed of the sea. Never again did he attempt to cross to the little island and brave the anger and scorn of Yalewa-ni-cagi-bula.

THE BOUNDARY QUARREL

OVALAU is a lovely island in the midst of the Fiji group. On it was built the old capital, Levuka, and in a valley behind the hills lies a village named Lovoni.

Rakavono was the ancestor god of this place. One day while at work building a house in the forest at some distance from the village, he realised that there was something wrong. It was a sixth sense that told him this, and he obeyed it.

"What has happened?" he asked as soon as he reached his home.

"Buisavulu, the goddess of Bureta has been here," he was told.

"What did she want?"

"She put a peg near the village to mark the boundary of her land," the people said.

"Oh! She did, did she?" said Rakavono. He went straight to the peg, pulled it out, broke it into small pieces, and threw them at Buisavulu.

The goddess was angry, and vowed vengeance on Rakavono, who had returned to the forest and continued to build his house. While he was working there he thought he heard an unusual sound, so he stopped and listened. The noise was the sound of water. He ran through the trees and looked down into the valley, where a strange sight met his eyes. Buisavulu was walking up towards Lovoni with the sea at her heels. It followed her up the valley, filling it from side to side; but when it reached Rakavono's village it turned towards the houses instead of going on up the foot of the hills.

Rakavono picked up three spears and ran quickly to the village, reaching it just as the waters began to wash round the houses. There were three creatures swimming in it, but of Buisavulu there was no sign. She had turned herself into three separate forms – a shark, a turtle, and a sailfish.

Rakavono recognised her at once.

"Ha! Is that you, Buisavulu?" he asked. "I shall spear you. If I miss, you may do what you like. If I miss you, you may go on through the forest to the very top of the valley and drown my village – but if I hit you – ha! – if I hit you!"

He sharpened his three spears by rubbing them on a rock, and

Buisavalu walked up to Lovoni with the sea at her heels.

then he took aim. The first spear shot through the air into the shark's body, which sank dead to the bottom of the water and was changed into a stone.

He picked up a second spear, aimed it, and hit the turtle. It also sank to the bottom of the raging water and became a stone.

Then Rakavono took his third spear, aimed it at the sail-fish killed it, and like its companions it settled beneath the water as a stone.

As soon as Buisavulu was killed in the form of these three creatures of the sea, the waters began to recede. They ebbed away as far as Bureta, leaving the valley dry as it had been previously.

One of Rakavono's men came up to him and said, "Sir, why don't you like the sea?"

"The sound of it is a nuisance in the night. None of us would ever be able to sleep with the noise of the sea in our ears all the time."

And so the village of Lovoni was saved from the sea. But the three stones still remain. One is shaped like a shark, one like a turtle, and the other like a fish. If you look closely you can also see the rock where Rakavono sharpened his spears.

NO SHELLFISH OR PARROTS IN BURETA

ONCE upon a time many parrots lived in the trees of Bureta on Ovalau, and there were plenty of shellfish in the streams; but today there are none at all. This is the reason.

In those far-off days the women used every day to dive for shellfish in the stream. They shouted and laughed as they gathered the shellfish, and made so much noise that the Women Ancestor Spirit grew angry. Her name was Buisavulu. She was a powerful spirit, for her father had been the great Rokomautu himself.

"Keep quiet, you women," Buisavulu ordered. "My children are asleep, I don't want you to wake them."

The women took no notice. They kept on shouting and talking at the top of their voices. Buisavulu was so angry that she said, "No more shellfish in this stream for ever and ever."

She was so powerful that what she said came true. The stream is there still – a beautiful stream, with waterlillies growing on it, pink and purple and white, but the shellfish have gone. Buisavulu sent them away to the Rewa river on Viti Levu.

Buisavulu could not stand noise of any kind. The parrots that flew from tree to tree were so beautiful, with their red and green feathers, but she couldn't bear to listen to the noise they made.

"Ka-ka, ka-ka." they called, all day long.

"No more parrots in this place!" Buisavulu said – and the moment she had said it, the parrots were whisked away, and appeared at Bau, another island many miles away. They do say that if anyone takes a parrot to Bureta it dies at once, because Buisavulu still can't bear the noise it makes.

THE FISH OF THE SWAMP

In the bay of Masomo on Vanua Balavu there is a fish called yawa, which has the sweetest flesh of all the fish in the world. It lives in a swamp where there is no water, but a great expanse of liquid mud. It is found only at this place and in Tonga.

Long ago a goddess of Tonga fell in love with the god of Laucala in Vanua Levu. She wondered what present would be most fitting for her lover, and decided that there was nothing he would appreciate so much as the yawa, which could be obtained on one of the smaller islands of Tonga. She wove a basket of leaves, caught some of the fish, and placed them inside the basket. Putting it under her arm she flew into the air and began the long journey over the sea towards Fiji.

The fish were not very comfortable in the basket, especially as they knew they were destined for the cooking oven on arrival. They wriggled about until they had made a small hole in the bottom of the basket, and soon had enlarged it sufficiently for them to make their escape.

One of the fish said, "Come, my brothers, let us be bold. If we work our way through the hole we shall fall into the sea, and so swim back to our home."

He led the way, and the others followed quickly; but at that moment the goddess happened to be flying over Vanua Balavu, and they fell to the ground and were unable to reach the sea.

When the goddess arrived at Laucala she greeted her lover, and opened her basket to show him the fish she had brought. She was greatly distressed to find that all it contained were a few leaves and fish scales and some mud. Of the fish there was no sign; but the hole at the bottom showed how they had escaped.

The god of Laucala was angry, thinking that she had made a fool of him. He spoke harshly to her and drove her away. The goddess flew back to her home weeping bitterly. As she passed over Masomo Bay her tears fell to the ground, where the fish were gasping for breath. The ground was moistened and turned to mud. The tears were not sufficient to form a pool, but the yawa were able to survive by burrowing into the liquid mud.

The only sign that the goddess ever visited Laucala is the fish scales that were emptied out of her basket and turned into flakes of mica; but at Masomo the yawa flourished, and have become a prized food of chiefs and kings.

As a gift from the gods they are cherished. Once every three years they are caught, but there are many sacred rites to be observed, lest the goddess of Tonga should be offended.

The men of Vanua Balavu paddle their canoes round to the bay and climb the hill until they come to the marsh. A hut is made for the priest, yaqona is prepared, the ovens are made ready, and the evening meal is eaten, after which the people go quietly to sleep.

At sunrise yaqona is again prepared and offered to the goddess. The people take logs of wood to keep themselves afloat in the mud, and wade out till their feet no longer touch the solid ground.

The priest, who is standing outside his shelter, calls out, "Ulia!" and the people stir up the mud with their long poles.

Again he calls, "Ulia!" and again the mud is stirred up.

A third time he cries, "Ulia!" and at this signal the yawa begin to jump out of the marsh. There is great excitement among the people. They call out, "The ship has come from Tonga!" and as the fish leap in the air they are caught in small nets and even in the hands, and thrown on to the bank.

The yawa, which are two or three feet long, are then divided between the king and the priest; and, as everyone knows, they are found only at Masomo in Vanua Balavu and on one of the islands of Tonga.

CHAPTER XI
LEGENDS OF BIRDS AND INSECTS

HOW THE CRABS DECEIVED THE HERON

Heron stalked majestically through the shallow water looking for small fish for his evening meal. Now and again he stopped to look at the crabs who were scuttling about looking for food and popping in and out of their holes. Heron burst into loud laughter.

"What ridiculous little creatures you are!" he exclaimed. "If I took tiny steps like you I would never get any food."

"We do very well, thank you." one of the crabs replied tartly. "Our food lies close to our burrows, but if we want to, we can run as quickly as you."

Heron bent down and looked at him curiously. "You are vain as well as funny," he said. "Don't you know that I can fly as well as walk? If I want to go a long distance I have only to flap my wings and glide into the air; and before you could scamper into your nasty damp little burrows I should be out of sight."

"So you say," Crab replied rudely.

"I'll prove it, too," Heron snapped. "I'll challenge you to a race tomorrow, from here to the coconut trees at the end of the beach – see them growing there by the rocks?"

"Of course I can see them!" Crab pushed out his eye-stalks and looked where Heron was pointing his long beak. From his lowly position he could see the feathery tops silhouetted against the sky. "You come here at sunrise and I'll be ready."

Heron stalked away. As soon as he was gone Crab felt rather foolish at having challenged so great a bird.

"What shall I do?" he asked his friends. "I've told Heron that I can race him to the palm trees, but I'd be worn out long before I got there, and anyway he can fly six times faster than I can run."

"We'd better have a meeting," they said, seeing that the honour of the crabs was at stake.

By the light of a moon that turned the sand to silver the crabs gathered in their hundreds and sat in a great circle clicking their claws and listening to the speakers. It was old Grandfather Crab who found the solution, and brought a frenzied round of clicking that drowned even the lapping of the waves on the shore and the dull boom of the surf on the reef.

The next day Crab and Heron stood at the edge of the tide.

Many of Heron's friends had come to watch the race.

"Where are your friends and relations?" asked Heron.

Crab waved his claw airily. "At home."

"Don't they want to see the race?"

"Not really. They're so sure I'll win that they aren't interested."

Heron clattered his beak. "Perhaps they're frightened that you're going to make a fool of yourself?"

"Well, we'll see. Let's not waste time talking."

Crab ran off. Heron could not move for laughing at his peculiar sideways manner of running. Presently Crab was lost to sight.

"You'd better get going," said one of the herons. "He runs rather faster than I thought."

"Don't worry. Half a dozen strokes of my wings and I'll overtake him."

He took a few steps, spread his wings and took off with such grace that his friends broke into applause, clapping their wings like hands, and shouting approval. Heron flew low over the beach, keeping a sharp look out of Crab, but could not see him anywhere.

"Funny!" he said to himself.

He flew on. Still there was no sign of Crab. "I must have outdistanced him already." he thought. "He couldn't possibly have got ahead of me."

But the further he flew, the more worried he became. "If I put my head down on the sand I will be able to hear him running, and I'll know whether he's in front of me or not," he thought.

No sooner was his head on the sand than a crab popped his head out of a hole.

"You!" exclaimed Heron. "What are you doing here?"

"Having a rest," Crab said cheerfully. "You fly on and I'll catch you up later."

Heron was thinking furiously as he strained his wing muscles, speeding through the air like an arrow. Twice he descended, and each time Crab put his head out of a hole near the tide level. Finally, with a despairing cry, Heron fluttered over to the trees and was greeted by the grinning face of Crab! He fell off the rocks into the sea and floated away on the ebb tide, while hundreds of tiny crabs came out of their burrows and laughed and danced and clicked their claws with glee.

What a pity Heron never knew that every crab he had seen was a different one! But then Crab has so many friends and relations that there's one for every hole in the sand and the mud on every island of Fiji.

THE CRANE AND THE BUTTERFLY

In Fiji cranes may often be seen walking on their long thin legs on the sandy beaches of the outer islets of the Lau archipelago, which is the part of Fiji nearest to Tonga.

One day a brightly coloured butterfly was flitting about in the hot sunshine near a sandy beach, when it saw a tall white crane stalking proudly along the shore.

"I can fly better than you can," the butterfly said proudly.

"Ah! – but I could fly much further than you," replied the crane.

"How far could you fly?" asked the butterfly.

"Well, I could fly all the way to Tonga!" boasted the crane.

"But Tonga is four hundred miles away!"

"Perhaps it would be too far for you, little butterfly," the crane sneered.

The butterfly was offended.

"I'll show you," she said. "We will have a race, and see who can get to Tonga first."

"Don't be so ridiculous," said the crane, "you could not possibly fly four hundred miles."

"Oh yes, I could. I'm starting now, and if you don't hurry you'll be left behind."

It was a lovely day. The sun shone brightly and the sea sparkled in the sunshine. The butterfly and the crane flew up and out over the lagoon. As they did so, the butterfly fluttered above the crane and alighted softly on his back.

The crane flew on with steadily beating wings. Every now and again he looked back to see if the butterfly was in sight, and felt quite pleased when he could not see her.

Hour after hour went by. The crane grew tired, but there was nowhere for him to alight, so he struggled on, until at last he saw land ahead.

"Poor butterfly!" he thought to himself. "Perhaps she has become tired and is struggling in the sea!"

The reefs passed slowly beneath him. But just before he reached the shore he saw something fluttering a few yards ahead of him and come to rest on the sand. It was the butterfly – who had reached Tonga before him.

WHY THE ROOSTER CROWS
WHEN THE TIDE IS RISING

MANY years ago all the fowls of Fiji were the subjects of a giant fowl whose name was Toatoatavaya-O. One day the chief fowl called upon his subjects to accompany him to the reef to gather the juicy clams and shellfish that were found on a large patch which became dry at low tide.

Spreading their wings, the fowls flew in a long line behind the leader until they came to the reef.

When they reached it, Toatoatavaya-O strode about proudly, pecking at all the choicest morsels and the fattest worms, gobbling them greedily before any of the other hens had a chance to snap them up. He strode about with his head in the air, and inadvertently placed one of his feet in the shell of a clam which was lying with the two halves wide open.

Immediately the clam closed its shell, and Toatoatavaya-O's foot was caught.

The tide was rising slowly; it crept up Toatoatavaya-O's legs, and then up to his body, and presently it reached his neck. He was terrified and struggled to free himself, but he was caught fast to the reef. In terror and desperation he begged the clam to let him go.

"Let go of my foot," he begged. "Perhaps you don't know who I am, but I am the chief of all the fowls, and the time has come to lead my subjects back to land. Hurry up and let me go, or I shall be drowned."

The clam opened its shell just enough to allow him to speak without releasing his grip on Toatoatavaya-O's leg.

"Why did you come to steal the worms and the shellfish from my reef?" it asked. "You belong to the land. This is a place for shellfish, and fish, and sea birds, but not for roosters. I don't think I will let you go."

"Let me go! Let me go!" the frantic rooster screeched. The other fowls flew round and round him, wildly calling his name and begging him to come home with them.

"Toatoatavaya-O!" they called, "Toatoatavaya-O!"

The tide rose steadily, until at last the poor chief of all the

He inadvertently placed his foot in the shell of a clam.

fowls was drowned. And to this very day the roosters crow and the hens cackle while the tide is rising.

Do you know what they say? They still call, "Toatoatavaya-O!" which is their way of saying cockadoodledoo.

HOW MOSQUITOES CAME TO ONEATA

In the days when the Great Serpent of Kauvadra brought the flood that drowned the Boat Builders, twelve men tied themselves to a tree trunk and drifted away on the flood waters. Eventually the tree trunk came ashore on the island of Kabara with ten men still alive. The dead men had been eaten by sharks.

Because they were famous for their skill at building canoes, the survivors were made welcome. They were given houses and women and set to work to make the first canoe that had ever been seen in the Lau Islands. They spent two years hollowing out the logs and carving them in pleasing designs to make a double canoe, which they furnished with sails and paddles.

They were two happy years, with interesting work to be done while their new-born children began to grow up in their own homes. They had only one complaint: every night they were plagued by mosquitoes. Their wives were kept busy during the hours of daylight beating the bark of the malo tree into the fine cloth called gatu, to keep the mosquitoes out.

Tuwara, the chief of Kabara, could hardly wait to launch the canoe that the Boat Builders had made for him. The builders went on board to sail the vessel, and Tuwara took many of his people with him. The sail was hoisted and the canoe glided over the still water, through the gap in the reef, and out into the open sea. The wind sang through the rigging, and the canoe surged merrily across the waves.

But Tuwara and his people began to feel unhappy. They no longer sang for joy, but lay on the deck and groaned, for the motion of the canoe made them sick.

"What is happening to us, Boat Builders?" asked Tuwara. "Our soul has left us, and our bellies are loose within us. What shall we do?"

Malani, the oldest Boat Builder, comforted him. "It is the sickness known as sea sickness," he said. "After a while it passes, but while it is still with a man, he wishes for death. My lord, the sickness will pass. And while we speak together we travel over the waves faster than a man can run."

Later in the day Malani came to the chief again.

"My lord, there is land ahead. Shall we go there, or would you rather sail on?"

Tuwara lifted his head wanly and groaned. "Beach the canoe at once, Malani. My soul has left my body, and I am a dead man if I cannot soon stand on land which does not roll and toss like palm trees in a hurricane."

The canoe grated on the sand of Oneata, and the people of Kabara staggered ashore. They were made welcome by the chief and stayed there many days and were content.

On that fair island there were no mosquitoes, so their nights were spent in unusual comfort, while during the day they feasted on the succulent shellfish known as kekeo.

After some time they left the island for their home, reluctantly, taking Wakuli-kulu, lord of Oneata, with them on a visit of state. On arrival he was feasted and taken to Tuwara's house. The two chiefs retired together. To the visitor's surprise, Tuwara drew a gaily painted curtain round their bed.

"What is it for?" the Oneata lord asked. "It is a beautiful piece of cloth, but why do we have to have it drawn around us?"

Tuwara was embarrassed, because he had kept the mosquito plague a secret from the other, and he sought for an excuse.

"It is useful and ornamental," he replied. "When a wind blows it shelters me." And with that his visitor had to be satisfied.

Presently a shrill drone filled the house.

"What is that?" Wakuli-kulu asked.

Tuwara was waiting for the question. He chuckled and said, "Ah, those are my tame mosquitoes."

"Mosquitoes? What are they?"

"They are little flying insects which come inside the house at night to sing me to sleep."

"What a wonderful thing this is!" Wakuli-kulu exclaimed.

He lay back and listened to the throbbing music. Presently he nudged Tuwara.

"What is it?" Tuwara asked sleepily.

"Tuwara, these insects delight my soul. Will you give them to me?"

"No, my friend, that is one thing I cannot do. My people would be angry if I gave away the treasure of our island."

"You could spare me at least some of them. Give me a few mosquitoes, and my people will remember you with gratitude."

"Even that is beyond my power, Wakuli-kulu. You see, these mosquitoes are affectionate creatures who cannot be parted from each other. If some of them went away the rest would follow. No, my very dear friend, much as I should like to grant your request, my people would never forgive me if I gave away the treasure of our land, and got nothing in return."

Wakuli-kulu brightened up. "Tuwara, my companion and my friend, there is nothing on my island that I would not give you for your singing insects."

Tuwara considered. "Wakuli-kuli, there is only one thing that would compensate my people for the loss of their mosquitoes."

"What is that?"

"The kekeo that live on your beaches. They are delicious. We have none on this island."

Wakuli-kulu made up his mind quickly. "It is a bargain, Tuwara. This is an exchange of presents between chiefs, between gods."

They went to sleep, but before daylight Wakuli-kulu woke up and began to pull the curtains aside. Tuwara sprang to his feet and jerked him back.

"What are you doing?"

The lord of Oneata had a beatific smile on his face.

"I love these insects you have given me. I want to see what they are like."

"You mustn't do that," Tuwara exclaimed in alarm.

"Why not?"

"You must *never* look at them. They are shy, modest. If they know they are being watched they will not sing."

Wakuli-kulu released the curtains and lay down again. When he woke the second time the sun was shining and the mosquitoes had disappeared.

While the men of Oneata prepared the canoe, ready to take the chief of Oneata home, Tuwara gathered all the mosquitoes together, by some means known only to the gods, and shut them in a large basket covered with fine mats.

As soon as the canoe with its strange freight reached Oneata, Wakuli-kulu sprang ashore and addressed his people.

"Great is our love for Tuwara and the people of Kabara. They have presented us with their greatest treasure, the singing insects of the night. Now we will go to sleep each night lulled by these wonderful mosquitoes. In return I have promised to give them our shellfish."

The people were excited by the news. They gathered the shellfish until not one was left on the beach, and loaded them on to the canoe.

Although night was falling, Tuwara ordered the sail to be hoisted at once. The canoe had not gone far before they heard a cry of anguish. Tuwara and his men grinned at each other. The impatient people of Oneata had opened the baskets and the mosquitoes had swarmed fiercely out, singing their song of defiance, and mercilessly biting the astonished villagers.

It was because of the cunning of Tuwara and the stupidity of Wakuli-kulu that Oneata has no kekeo and is troubled by myriads of mosquitoes, while the people of Kabara sleep untroubled at night, and feed on succulent shellfish by day.

CHAPTER XII
LEGENDS OF ANIMALS

HOW DAU-LAWAKI ATE THE SACRED CAT

DAU-LAWAKI, the Great Rogue, was strong in soul, ruthless, egotistical, and overbearing. When a party of Tongan warriors, who had been helping the men of Lakeba in their battles, returned to their own land, he went with them.

He had not been long in the village of Haapai before he was interested to hear everyone speaking of Alo-alo, the god who lived in the village temple.

"What is so wonderful about your god?" he asked.

They were anxious to tell him.

"Let us begin at the beginning. Alo-alo has always been our god, but a little while ago he came here to live amongst us. One day we saw a strange canoe anchored off shore, and we planned to capture it and destroy the crew. We were to attack at dawn; but when the light came, and the men were ready to launch the canoes, we found that the bay was empty. The canoe must have left during the night. This made us angry. Some accused others of having warned the strangers. We came to blows, and some men were killed. It was a sad day for the women at Haapai.

"The next morning the high priest went to the temple of Alo-alo to ask the god why he was angry with us. We gathered in the square to hear the words of Alo-alo. Presently the priest came running out of the temple, shaking with fright.

" 'Listen,' he said. 'Listen to me, men and women of Haapai. The god has not spoken – he has appeared and showed me his sacred body. I have seen Alo-alo. He comes!'

"Then the god appeared in his true form. He walked out of the temple and sat down. We feared lest he had come to punish us, but he looked on us with favour. So we have fed the god and his priest, and they grow fat. While he remains with us, we shall prosper."

"Let me see your god who walked among you," said Dau-lawaki.

"You must reverence him, and he will show himself to you," they warned him. "Come with us."

They took Dau-lawaki to the square and told him to watch the temple. Presently a black shadow appeared, and a cat stalked out, sat down and yawned in the sunshine.

"Alo-alo, Alo-alo!" the people cried, while the Fijian stared in astonishment.

"Is *that* your god?"

"Yes – in truth, it is our great Alo-alo."

"Then Alo-alo is a cat," Dau-lawaki said. He smiled secretly, for he had not eaten flesh for a while, and craved the flesh of the cat who had become a god. He knew that he could not take it openly, but planned to take it by subtlety, for he knew that it could do him no harm.

One night a voice was heard crying repeatedly in the temple. The people woke up and assembled in the square, asking each other in awed tones what had happened.

The priest came out. "Be quiet, men of Haapai. Listen! The god will speak."

A hush fell on the crowd. In the silence they heard a deep voice, speaking in another tongue, but one that was recognisable.

"Deliver the cat to the Fijian that he may eat it."

The chiefs gathered together as the people dispersed, and debated the matter. In the morning they were all called together by the beating of a drum, and the cat was brought out with its paws bound tightly.

"Come forth, Dau-lawaki," the priest cried.

The Fijian stepped forward with a puzzled expression.

"We have discussed a wonderful thing together, Dau-lawaki," the priest said. "The wonder is outside our understanding. Alo-alo has spoken to us, but his words were in another tongue – in Fijian. Alo-alo is a god of Tonga, not of Fiji. But his words were plain. He has told us that the cat, that is his very self, must be killed and cooked and given to you. He is our god, we are his people, and we must obey. We dare not kill the cat. You must kill it yourself, Dau-lawaki."

The Fijian was pushed forward. He was shaking like a palm-frond in the wind.

"Spare me," he cried, "I dare not touch the body of the god."

"If you will not do what the god has commanded, we shall have to sacrifice you to him."

With seeming reluctance Dau-lawaki killed the cat, and gave it to the young men to cook; later he ate his meal with obvious enjoyment.

After the bones were buried within the confines of the temple, the Fijian begged to be allowed to return to his own country, lest the anger of the god should descend on him. A canoe was manned, and he was returned to Fiji.

Not one word had he spoken to the Tongans about the eating

"Is *that* your god?"

of the cat. Great was their shame when they heard him tell his friends how he had pretended to be a god and had eaten the sacred cat, which they believed to be the physical presence of Alo-alo. And greater still was their shame when they heard the children of Lakeba shouting, "Deliver the cat to the Fijian that he may eat it."

As soon as they could they left for their own land. One thing, however, was certain, Dau-lawaki never showed his face again in Tonga.

THE RAT AND THE FLYING FOX

STRONG wings and beauty are not nearly as important as a quick mind, as Rat once proved to Heron. Watching the graceful bird flapping its lazy way over the lagoon, Rat looked down at his own short little legs in disgust.

"If only I had the heron's wings," he mused. "And why shouldn't I?"

He put his front paws in his mouth and whistled shrilly. Heron faltered in his flight, looked down, and saw Rat standing on his hind legs on the white coral beach. He circled round slowly, gliding down lower, until he stood in front of Rat.

"What are you doing, Rat? What do you want?"

Rat giggled. "I was thinking how dull it must be for you, having to fly wherever you want to go."

"That was kind of you," Heron said sarcastically. "I would have thought that you would gladly exchange your four short legs for my lovely wings."

"No, no," laughed Rat. "Up there in the sky you can't see anything properly. You're too far away from all the interesting things that live on the earth."

"What sort of things?"

"Oh – berries, and insects, and birds' eggs – no, I didn't mean that. I mean good things to eat."

Heron laughed. "You've never been up there, Rat. I look down on the earth and the sea as if I were a god. I can see the colour of the coral through the clear water. I can see fish and shellfish."

Rat's mouth watered, but he twirled his whiskers proudly.

"Heron," he said, "you have never crept under the cool shade of the banana trees, or tunnelled in the soft moist earth. You have never raced through the long pathways and felt the earth rushing past under your feet and the whisper of the undergrowth where insects live their busy lives, where the frond of drooping plants and trees brush your fur with tender fingers. You can only plod on through the air, blinded by the sun, with nothing but empty sea below you."

"You talk too much, Rat," said Heron. He flapped his wings and lifted his feet from the ground. "Who'd want to scuttle through nasty damp undergrowth listening to worms and insects slithering about in the mould? Why, I can soar through the air faster than the wind. I could fly to that tree, and go to sleep for a little while and get to the end of the beach before you, no matter how fast you ran!"

"I don't think you could, Heron."

"I say I could, and what's more I will! I'll give you the biggest feed of fish you ever had in your life if you get there first."

"Don't care much for fish," Rat replied. "Still, to show you that I can run faster than you think, I'll do my best. But you won't forget to have a sleep under that tree, will you?"

"Of course not," laughed Heron. "Off you go."

Rat set off, running as fast as he could. He could feel his heart beating quickly, not with running, but with excitement. He had a long way to run, and the sun was directly overhead when he came in sight of the tree. His racing heart missed a beat, because he could not see Heron; but as he came closer he saw the bird dozing in the shade of the tree. He tiptoed up and asked softly, "Are you awake?"

There was no reply. Heron was sleeping soundly. Rat crept up to the bird and began to nibble the base of its wings gently, oh so gently. Heron stirred in his sleep and settled down again. Presently one wing was lying on the ground. Rat began work on the other, and when he was finished he dragged them into the undergrowth. He searched until he found strong pliant creepers with which he lashed the wings to his own legs.

Heron was lying in the same place, still asleep in shadow; but the sun was gradually creeping up its body as it sank towards the west. Rat ran along the sand, spread the borrowed wings, and in a moment of ecstasy felt his feet leaving the ground. He flapped vigorously and, cushioned on the yielding air, he soared upwards and clung to a thin branch at the top of the tree.

Looking down, he watched as the sunlight slid up Heron's face. The bird blinked in the strong light, stood up, and peered down the beach.

"Dear me, I have slept longer than I thought," Rat heard him murmur. "I wonder where that wretched Rat has got to?"

He ran lightly along the sand, tried to stretch out his wings, and discovered they were gone. The bird sat down suddenly, wondering what had happened. There was still no sign of Rat, but when he looked down he saw the marks of the animal's paws. He stood up and followed them back, until he came to a place where the footprints were scarcely discernible, and then faded away.

"Funny," said Heron, "where can he have gone?"
"Here," twittered Rat.
"Where? Where are you?"
"Up in the tree!"
"How did you get there?"
"Easily, Heron. I borrowed a pair of wings. Look!"

He flew out of the branches, out and across the lagoon, and back to his perch.

"Come back with my wings," Heron screamed, furious at his loss. "You don't want them. You said how much better it was running through the undergrowth!"

"I know, I know. I'm such a generous soul that I want you to have that pleasure. I shall be quite content to fly around like this."

He flew out of sight and perched on another tree – the first of all the flying foxes of Fiji. Poor Heron ran into the shelter of the broad-leaved plants. Sometimes his friends looked for him, but he was never seen again. Perhaps he can be found looking for insects and berries in the forest on dark nights, but no one knows. Perhaps he died of sorrow and shame when Rat stole his wings and changed himself into a flying fox.

WHY PIGS DIG FOR WORMS

VEGETABLES cooked in an earth oven are fit for men and gods only when placed in baskets with succulent steaming meat, rich with fat, on top. Then a man may take taro or yam or green leaves in one hand, a piece of flesh in the other, and feast as though he were a god. The only difficulty is to find an animal that can be steamed or roasted and that will provide enough flesh for a hungry man to eat. Birds and rats are far too small.

"Let us ask the gods," men said.

They started up the mountain to make their request, and were accompanied by fish, reptiles, animals, birds, and insects, all interested in hearing the answer.

The gods, who also like good food, were in a receptive mood and welcomed this strangely assorted deputation. They looked round the assembly speculatively, and many a bird and animal cowered in a corner, hoping not to be noticed.

One of the gods reached out and caught Rat by the scruff of the neck and held him. The poor animal fought and twisted, and in his squealing voice cried, "Not me! Not me! I am too small. I'm all bones, and I don't taste at all nice. Let me go!"

"Yes, he is too small," the men said. "We need a much bigger animal than Rat."

"What about Pig?" one of the gods suggested. "Now there's a fine animal for you – rich and savoury."

Pig was pulled out by his short tail and stood shivering in front of them.

"I am too big," he squealed. "You could never get me into one of your baskets."

"Perhaps you are right," another god said, "but perhaps you are wrong." He addressed the man.

"Fill a basket and put Pig on top and you can see what he looks like."

The protesting pig was dumped on to a basket. His legs fitted inside comfortably, but his snout stuck out at one end and his tail at the other.

Pig had a broad smile on his face.

"What did I tell you?" he said smugly.

Rat, who was still congratulating himself on his escape, rushed forward, twisted the tail into a spiral and tucked it inside the basket.

Pig still had a broad smile on his face.

"What did I tell you?" he said smugly. "You've got my tail inside but you'll never get me properly into the basket. My snout is too long."

Worm wriggled himself upright until he was balanced on his coiled tail.

"What is it, Worm?"

"Please, if we were to break Pig's snout we could bend it up and then he would fit into the basket."

And that's what they did. Which explains why Pig has a turned-up nose. It also explains why he spends so much time digging up the ground looking for worms!

CHAPTER XIII
LEGENDS OF FLOWERS AND FRUIT

HOW SERUA GOT ITS NAME

OFF the southern coast of Viti Levu there is an island called Serua. Hundreds of years ago some Fijians who lived amongst the mountains on the north-western side of Viti Levu decided to journey southwards to the coastal regions. Men, women, and children descended the tracks between the jungle grasses and shrubs and along the river valleys, crossing the mountain spurs and walking beside the streams in the lower valleys.

After climbing a long hill and reaching the summit, they were surprised to see a wide expanse of ocean. It was a sight they had never seen before from their deep valleys in the interior of the island.

"Let us go down to the shore," they cried.

When they came to the beach they looked across the water and saw a beautiful island close to the shore.

"Just look at it," they cried. "Look at that beautiful island. Let us go there."

They cut bamboo stems, lashing them together with strong vines, and made a raft which they poled across to the island. It was uninhabited, and a wonderful place in which to live.

"We will stay here," they said, and began to explore the place, pushing their way through the luxurious growth of bushes and vines.

One of them called to a friend, "Look at this lovely flower – it has only two petals."

"Se i rua," they said, "only two petals."

Some of the families remained on the island, collecting posts and thatching-leaves, and reeds and roofing-poles from the forests, and built strong houses. The others returned to Viti Levu. They went up the river valleys and over the mountains, back to the hill district from which they had come.

The people who stayed behind lived happily on Serua, the island that is named after the two-petalled flower.

THE TAGIMOUCIA FLOWERS

TAVIUNI is a lovely island with fertile soil where all plants grow splendidly. Not only is there a luxuriant growth of coconuts and food crops, but the flowers on that island bloom in all the pride of their beauty.

On a hill above the sea shore on the island of Taviuni lived a mother and her daughter. One day the little girl was disobedient, playing when she should have been working. Although her mother kept on asking her to get on with her work, she took no notice. At last her mother's patience gave out.

"You naughty girl!" she said. "You naughty girl!" She seized the bundle of coconut leaf midribs which she used as a broom, and hit her daughter with it.

"I disown you," she said. "Get out. Go somewhere where I can't see you. I never want to see your face again."

The little girl cried and ran away. She kept on running, not knowing where she was going. Her eyes full of tears, she blundered into a big climbing plant that hung from a tree. It was a large ivi tree, over which a vine had grown and hung right down to the ground. It had a thick soft green stem and large green leaves, but there were no flowers on it. The little girl became completely tangled up in the vine, and couldn't get free, so she hung there, still crying bitterly.

As the tears rolled down her cheeks they changed from salt water to tears of blood, that fell on the stems of the vine and became lovely flowers.

And there they are to this day. The people of Taviuni and of other places remember that these flowers originated in the tears of the little girl. They call them Tagi-mo-uci-au, because this is what they would have liked to have said if they had been there and seen the little girl crying. The tagimoucia flowers bloom at the edge of a lagoon near the beaches of Taviuni.

As for the little girl, she finally managed to struggle free from the vine and went back to her home. She stopped crying the moment she found that her mother had forgotten her anger, and so they lived happily again in their home. But the terrible experience that happened to her that day will always be remembered while tagimoucia flowers bloom on Taviuni.

She kept on running not knowing where she was going.

THE LOST ORANGE

LONG before white people came to Fiji, the young men used to play ball games with oranges. There was a young chief of Nasowata who was fond of games of this kind, and often played with young men of his own age.

While they were playing one day they lost the orange, and were upset to find that there were no more oranges in the village. They searched everywhere for the lost ball, but in vain.

The principal chief of the village said to his people, "This orange must be found. I can't let my son be disappointed. It is all right for common people, but my son must have his own way. Get to work, you lazy fellows, and find that orange quickly."

They searched everywhere, but there was no sign of it. They came back again to the old chief and reported in fear and trembling.

He stood up frowning.

"My son must have his orange! I will give a reward to the one who finds it. If it is a girl who discovers it, she shall have the chance of marrying my son. If it is a boy who finds it, I will divide my land into two equal parts; one of them of course will go to my son, but the other to the young man who finds the orange."

He lay down on his mat, and went to sleep, smiling to himself, because he knew that his people would be kept very busy; but he had little fear that the orange would be found.

In another village, not far away, a young woman of high rank had decided to go fishing. She called her women attendants, and they went in canoes down the stream to the sea coast, taking fishing nets with them. When they reached the shore they caught a good supply of fish, which they piled high in the canoes, and they began to pole their way upstream. The women were wet and cold, but they were happy because they had been so successful.

Presently they saw an orange floating on the water. The chief's daughter said imperiously, "Get me that orange, I want to eat it." Two of the girls jumped out of the canoe, brought the orange, and gave it to the chief's daughter, who ate it at once.

It was not an important incident, but somebody mentioned it, and eventually the people of Nasowata heard that the high-born young woman of Rewa had found and eaten the missing orange.

The old chief of Nasowata remembered his promise, and

LEGENDS OF FLOWERS AND FRUIT 203

reflected that a marriage of his son to the daughter of the chief of Rewa would be a happy occurrence. He sent a message to her father, inviting him to give his daughter in marriage.

The chief of Rewa agreed, but the girl herself felt very differently about the offer. She had no love for the young chief of Nasowata. She called her girls together, and they fled out of the village, down to the river bank, stepped into a canoe, and slipped silently down the river. They were hidden by the high mango trees, and in silence they propelled the boat downstream until they came to the delta at the sea shore.

Two miles off shore on the outer reef lay the island of Nukulau, and it was felt that it would be a safe shelter from pursuit.

As they watched, a huge black wave rose above the canoe, blotting out the light and eclipsing the sun. Heedless of the darkness, they paddled the canoe onwards, but when the light returned they found that a large shark was following them. As they watched, it turned into a man, tall and ugly, who spoke to the chief's daughter.

"Don't be afraid, my grand-daughter, I have come to protect you from your troubles. Shut your eyes, all of you, and trust me."

The high-born woman and her attendants obediently shut their eyes, and a moment later they found themselves inside a Fijian house. Tapa cloths adorned the walls, and beautiful pandanus leaf mats were on the floor. Underneath them was clean, dry fern, and there was a sweet refreshing smell in the house. The girl's grandfather and grandmother were there to greet them, and they were all treated so well that they were content to stay there for ever.

But no one knows where that magic house is. It is not on the island of Nukulau at the entrance to Suva Harbour. It is hidden away somewhere where the young chief who likes playing games with oranges will never find it.

HOW BANANAS CAME TO FIJI

THERE was once a little girl who lived with her mother in a lonely house on top of a hill, far away from any village. The hill top was in Tailevu, on the eastern side of Viti Levu.

The mother was a selfish woman. She did not want her daughter to see other people, but preferred to keep her to herself. So the years passed by and the girl grew into a beautiful young woman. The mother was now more than ever determined to keep her away from the sight of others, and especially from young men who might desire her for themselves.

The house in which the mother and daughter lived was a beautiful one, large and airy, with great tree trunks for posts, and smaller tree trunks forming the framework of the roof, which was thatched with bracken fern. The walls were made of makita leaves, lined inside with reeds tied with coconut fibre sinnet. On the earthen floor, dried fern had been placed to a depth of several inches, and clean mats were spread on top. The few visitors who came loved the fragrant, clean smell of the house and enjoyed the breezes that were ever blowing through it.

The girl reached an age when she longed to see other places and people. She wondered what the rest of the world was like, but all that she could see were a few hills and trees, and the empty sky above them.

One day her mother went off to get fish. As she picked up her net and basket the girl said, "Please mother, may I go for a little walk outside while you are away?"

"Oh, very well," the mother replied, "but mind you are back before sunset."

The mother went down the hill to the sea shore. Her daughter wandered about, looking at the trees and flowers, and lost all sense of time. She climbed a hill and, feeling rather tired, sat down to rest. She had forgotten that she must be back by sunset, and was overtaken by darkness.

Suddenly a young man appeared before her.

"Who are you?" he asked. "Where do you live?"

"Sit down," the girl said laughingly, "and I'll tell you."

They sat together on the hill top and talked about many things. The time passed so quickly for them both that before they knew where they were, they heard a cock crowing in the distance. The girl jumped to her feet, and the young man stood up. He held out his hand in farewell. As she took it in hers he vanished, leaving his hand and his forearm in her grasp!

She stood for a while, lost in thought, and then walked back to her home and her mother. She related what had happened to her, and later in the day she planted the hand and arm in a patch of earth outside the house.

A few days later a shoot appeared above the ground. It grew quickly, and some months later a large reddish brown bud appeared; it was followed by small fruit which grew into a great bunch, shaped like the fingers of a hand. They were bananas. And that is how bananas came to Fiji.

THE VANISHING BREADFRUIT

FIJIANS are fond of breadfruit, which grows on trees with large glossy leaves. The big, round, green fruit is picked and cooked, and served with fish and coconut cream sauce, or with green vegetables; it is a welcome change from the ordinary diet of yam and dalo.

One day two Fijians were standing near a breadfruit tree which grew on the bank of a stream. The tree was reflected in the clear water, and the men thought how good it would be to have the fruit cooked with a tasty relish of fish or prawns and leaves.

One of them said, "We'll each have a share of the breadfruit. I'll take the top ones and you can have the bottom ones."

The second man, looking at the breadfruit mirrored in the water, dived in to gather his share; but when he got to the bottom of the stream, he found that the breadfruit had vanished.

The other meanwhile had quickly climbed up the tree, gathered all the fruit that was there, tied them on the two ends of a pole, slung it over his shoulder, and set off for home before his friend had time to get out of the water.

CHAPTER XIV
LEGENDS OF TREES AND PLANTS

THE GODS WHO EXCHANGED TREES

ON Cikobia there are many fruitful dawa trees, while on the neighbouring island of Munia flourishes the mamakara tree. It was not so in the beginning of time, for the dawa grew on Munia and the mamakara on Cikobia.

Rasikilau was the god of Cikobia. Oh, a powerful god – the ground shook as he walked and his head was far above the tree tops. He was lonely, until one day a canoe came from some far-off land towards the north. On board was a goddess of great beauty, who responded to his love.

Two boys were born to them. They inherited the good looks of their mother and the strength of their father. While they were still young they pulled up mamakara trees by the roots, and fashioned them into clubs. When they played the ball game they stood at the opposite ends of the island, throwing pebbles to each other and catching them in their hands. Children of other islands use the soft fruit of the dawa tree as balls, but as no dawa then grew on Cikobia, these two boys used pebbles that they found on the beach.

The boys were good friends, until one day they found a fish washed up on the beach, and quarrelled over who should have it. It was only big enough for a meal for one of them, and both were hungry. Neither would give way to the other, and in desperation one of them picked up a large rock and threw it at his brother.

Their father had been watching them from a distance. He saw the rocks flying through the air, thrown not in play but in anger. Occasionally one of the boys would be struck on the head, but the rocks bounced off harmlessly, or were smashed to pieces against their hard skulls.

Rasikilau was appalled by the sight, for he realised that if his sons had such strength while they were still boys, when they reached manhood they might injure him, or send him away from his home. He rushed up to them, caught them by the hair, and dashed their heads together with such force that they were both killed outright.

Then he remembered that their mother would be waiting for them to return, and he was afraid. He dared not tell her what had happened.

"Sobo!" said he, "I have sad news. From afar off I saw our

sons at play. After a while they quarrelled, and began to hurl rocks at each other. Now they are both dead, each killed by the other."

The goddess was overcome with grief. Day after day she stayed in her house, the tears running down her cheeks, and refused to be comforted. Rasikilau remained outside. His spirit was heavy, for the memory of his deed lay between him and his wife.

News of his distress came to Koroibo, the god of Munia Island. He was an old friend, and he thought that if he brought gifts with him he would be able to cheer up the god of Cikobia. Rasikilau greeted him and accepted the gifts, after which the gods sat together under the trees. Koroibo looked at the shady mamakara tree enviously, and wished that they grew on his own island. He listened as Rasikilau told him that his sons had met their death by throwing rocks at each other, and a crafty scheme came into his mind.

After the evening meal he said to his host, "My soul grieves at the death of your sons. If only you had had dawa trees growing here they could have played with the soft fruit, as my children do, and no harm could have come to them."

"That is true," Rasikilau replied, "but now it is too late. My sons are dead."

"Ah, but you may well have more. Your wife is still young and vigorous, and you need sons to comfort you. You should be prepared for that day. Listen, Rasikilau, I will give you all my dawa trees and there will be plenty of fruit on your island. All I ask in return is that you give me your mamakara trees."

"It is well," said Rasikilau.

They sat down and drank yaqona to signify that the exchange was acceptable. Then Rasikilau pulled up all his mamakara trees and loaded them into Koroibo's canoe, which was sent back again full of dawa trees.

So the mamakara trees grew in Munia in place of the dawa trees, and on Cikobia the dawa trees flourished where once the mamakara trees had grown. Koroibo was well satisfied, but Rasikilau had the worst of the bargain, because his wife still refused to be comforted. Presently her sorrowful spirit departed from her body, and could be heard sighing where her husband sat in lonely solitude under his dawa trees.

THE TURTLE NUTS OF THE VONU TREE

THE ancient ceremony of the calling of the turtles had been held for many years in the village of Nacamaki on the island of Koro. The people put flowers in their hair and leis of fragrant blooms around their necks, and on a certain day the whole village went down to the beach. For a long time they chanted songs and clapped their hands until, one after the other, the turtles swam up from the depths of the sea and crawled ashore. It was an amazing sight. The white sand suddenly became black with crawling turtles of all sizes, from tiny babies to the enormous veterans of many adventures.

As soon as the turtle invasion began it was the custom for the villagers to go back to their homes without a single backward glance, and to stay there for a night and a day, leaving the beach to the turtles. There was much speculation as to what happened there, but the ceremony was one that had been imposed upon their ancestors by the gods, and no one dared to break the tabu, until one inquisitive and sceptical man defied the ancient edict in order to satisfy his curiosity.

"This year I will find out what happens," he thought, "for if this law was made by the gods, it was so long ago that even they must have forgotten by now why they imposed it on us."

Then he was struck by a disquieting thought. "Why do the turtles all come ashore on the same day, and only after we have clapped our hands and sung our songs?"

He thought about this for a while, then shrugged his shoulders and consoled himself with the reflection that nothing was likely to happen to him, and that his curiosity could never be satisfied until he had learned the secret of the visit of the turtles.

When the day for the next ceremony arrived he made himself as inconspicuous as possible, and while the others were chanting with their eyes fixed on the sea, he stole away and hid in the mangrove trees close by the water's edge. It was a good position, for he was well concealed yet had a good view of the beach. Presently the first turtles appeared, followed by thousands of others who seemed to be coming in from every direction. He watched his friends turn around and obediently make their way back to the village. The turtles all came ashore and stood in

"Foolish mortal. Why are you hiding there?"

long rows on the sand with their heads towards the sea, as though they were watching for someone to come.

The inquisitive man turned his head and saw something that looked like a cloud coming rapidly in from the sea. It came closer, and through it he could dimly see a huge figure; but whether it was a man, a turtle, some mysterious denizen of the deep sea, or a god, he could not tell. To his surprise the apparition did not set foot on the beach. Gliding along the surface of the water, it turned aside and threaded its way between the mangrove trees until it was standing in front of him.

"Foolish mortal," a voice spoke out of the cloud. "Why are you hiding there? You know that the gods have forbidden men and women to look at the turtle tribe on the one day of the year when they assemble on the island of Koro. The others have returned to their homes. What are you doing here?"

The man tried to speak, but he was so frightened that his teeth chattered, and no words came out of his mouth.

"Never mind," the voice from the cloud said. "I can read your rebellious thoughts. Now you are afraid; but I know that when fear leaves you, sorrow will not take its place. The gods tell me that I must make an example of you, so that you will not live to see another turtle day, nor even to repent of the evil that you have done. The thing that will happen to you will be a reminder of your folly and a warning to your people that the will of the gods must be obeyed."

Two rigid arms flashed out of the mist and the frightened man was surrounded by a ribbon of light, which gleamed for a mometn and was gone. Gone too was the man, and on the spot where he had stood, a tree grew.

When their friend failed to return, the villagers wondered. They remained in their homes the next day, but on the third day they searched for him. He was never found; but the vonu tree, with the hard nuts that are like the shell of a turtle, was discovered, and again men wondered.

While vonu nuts grow on Koro Island no man will ever dare to try to find out what the turtles do when they come ashore near Nacamaki village.

HOW THE MOON WAS TRAPPED

In the province of Rewa, there were once two men who were great friends. One of them had come from Taci and the other from Nadoria. When the man from Taci found good food he would take it to his friend in Nadoria, and so they exchanged the things they valued most.

The villages were some two or three miles apart. One day the man from Taci brought food to his friend; they spent the evening eating it, telling each other stories. One of them then suggested that it would be a good thing to go out fishing that night, because the moon was shining so brightly. So they prepared their fishing gear and went down to the river to fetch the canoe, which they boarded and paddled downstream until they came to a popular fishing ground.

While they were fishing the man from Taci caught many fish, but his friend had no luck at all. Later in the evening the luck changed, and the man from Nadoria caught just one fish; but it was bigger than all his friend's put together. It was so large that they could not even tow it behind the canoe. They hauled the anchor up quickly, and allowed the fish to drag the canoe backwards and forwards until it was tired, after which they hauled it up and fastened it firmly to the canoe.

As they paddled back home an argument arose between them, as to who was to bake the fish. In those days it was usual to bake fish rather than boil it. Finally they agreed that the man from Taci would undertake the baking.

The two friends paddled their canoe all the way to Taci. As the man from Nadoria returned home he noticed how brightly the moon was shining. On arrival at his village he lay down and went to sleep, without telling his wife that he had caught the big fish.

The following day he still kept the news to himself. But in the evening he dressed himself in his best clothes and started on his journey. When he came close to his friend's village he heard the people shouting and laughing, and knew at once that they were having a feast. Then he met some boys and girls who were crunching fish bones in their teeth – and with a shock he realised they had been eating the very fish that he had caught the previous evening.

He entered the outskirts of the village and came to the house of his friend. He was not invited to eat any of the fish, but was simply given something to drink – and then he knew that the villagers had eaten all of his fish and left none for himself.

He went outside the house and called his friend.

"Is there any fish left?" he asked.

"No, you are too late, my friend, we have just finished eating it all up."

The man from Nadoria made no reply. He began to walk back to his own village, and while he was going along the track the moon rose. He was so angry that he determined to extinguish it, so that there would be no moonlight for the man of Taci nor for his descendants for evermore.

When he arrived home he told his wife everything that had happened, and advised her what he was going to do.

The next day he went up into the hills to get some bamboo and branches with which to construct a moon trap. He asked the men of a hill village to help him carry the materials back to his home. After they had cut them, they accompanied him, carrying long thick bamboos and branches of she-oak trees.

His wife made a pudding of coconut, taro, and sugar juice, while he constructed a huge trap from the bamboo stalks and the she-oak branches. Meanwhile the pudding was standing ready.

Unknown to her husband, the woman had prepared two large coconut shells, one of which contained salt water and the other fresh.

Then the man called the moon, which had risen above the horizon and was shining brightly.

"Moon, Moon," he called, "come and eat this lovely pudding."

The moon came down and began to eat the pudding. As he was doing so, the woman threw the bowl of fresh water in his face, and followed it up with the salt water. The moon was so startled that he jumped up and received a handful of mud in his face.

This was too much for the moon. He sprang upwards so quickly that the nokonoko or she-oak branches had no time to grasp him, and escaped and climbed back to his place in the sky.

The woman had not agreed with her husband's plan at any time; but like a wise woman, instead of arguing with him, she had prepared the coconut cups full of water and had thrown them at the moon, startling him so much that he made his escape.

She knew the value of moonlight, and having more common sense than her husband, she preserved the bright light of the night not only for her own descendants but for everyone else, including the greedy Taci people.

That is how the moon escaped from his trap. That is why so many nokonoko trees grow near the village of Nadoria.

HOW SUGAR CANE CAME TO ROTUMA

ON the small island of Uea, near the larger island of Rotuma, there lived a brother and sister who loved each other dearly. The girl's name was Rakitefurisia, and her brother's name Aiatos.

Uea is a small, high, rocky island. It is really a mountain the peak of which stands out above the sea, and is therefore not suitable for gardening. When the people of Uea needed to grow yams or bananas or dalo they had to make a journey by canoe across the sea to Rotuma.

When the time came for Aiatos to grow food he went alone to Rotuma, because it is the custom of Uean women to stay at home and not to work in the plantations. Aiatos had to work hard to prepare the ground for the plantation. He cut down the long grass and gathered it in a heap to burn. Then he made fire by rubbing a hard piece of wood briskly on a softer piece; when the spark appeared he caught it in a wisp of dry grass which he held in his hand, shielded it from the wind, and so carried it to the large pile of grass. He was glad to see that it was burning well, because he needed a large, clean piece of ground for the planting of yams.

The smoke from the bonfire went up into the sky, where it stung the eyes of the spirit people and annoyed them. When they found that they could not attract his attention they let down a great net and the unsuspecting Aiatos was caught in it and pulled upwards.

In the island of Uea, Rakitefurisia missed her brother. She had seen the smoke ascending and knew that he was hard at work. When she looked again she saw the net going steadily up into the sky with her brother caught in it.

"Aiatos! Aiatos!" she called at the top of her voice, "Come back, come back."

But Aiatos could not come back. Slowly the net went up until it disappeared from sight, and her brother was imprisoned in the spirit world. Rakitefurisia did not know what to do. She ran round and round the island, and then climbed up to the highest part of the mountain, to see whether she could not reach the sky to save her brother. When she got there, the sky still lay far above her. She sat down and cried, beating her heels up and down in her distress. In this way she made two depressions in the

The unsuspecting Aiatos was caught in the net and pulled upwards.

mountain which were later filled with water; these two ponds can be seen on Uea to this very day.

Aiatos was even more miserable than his sister. He found no comfort or joy in the spirit world of the sky, and longed to return to his home and his sister. The spirits had told him that whatever he did he must not open the windows of his spirit home, but at length he disobeyed them. In the skyland he had found some pieces of sugar cane, and these he tossed out of a window, so that they fell on to the island of Uea. They lay on the mountain top, close to where Rakitefurisia was beating her heels on the ground. Her eyes were so full of tears that she did not notice the sugar cane that had fallen behind her.

Aiatos also cried so much that the spirits grew tired of the sound of his voice.

"All right, Aiatos," they said, "we will be glad to get rid of you. Go quickly."

They lowered him in the net and he landed on the mountain peak of Uea. There was his sister, not far from him. He put out his arms to embrace her, but discovered that she had turned into dust. And as he embraced the image that had once been his beloved sister, he also turned into dusty soil.

A long time afterwards the people of Uea ascended the mountain. They saw the two heaps of dust, which were all that remained of Aiatos and Rakitefurisia, and behind them the pieces of sugar cane that had been thrown down from the spirit world in the sky.

They picked them up and took them over to the main island of Rotuma, where the soil was so much more fertile. There they were planted, and so sugar cane was introduced to Rotuma and grew in the food gardens, together with the yams and taro and cooking bananas. Whenever the people felt like it they would take a juicy length of sugar cane, peel off the bark and suck the sweet syrup, spitting out the white pith. This was the gift that the brother and sister gave them, and which has always remained on Rotuma.

HOW THE VIA PLANT WAS TAKEN TO REWA

IN the Rewa district where the streams move slowly to the coast there are many picturesque villages clustered along the shore; and near every village there will be found a patch of via plants. They grow in soil near brackish water, so that they are particularly useful as coastal plants. The root of the via is rather like a dalo, but is hard and has to be pounded with a flat mallet before it is cooked.

The via grew on the little island of Beqa long before it was known on the mainland of Viti Levu.

The people of Beqa are related to the people of Rewa. Long ago a young Rewa chief went fishing. He sailed his canoe out of the mouth of the river, across the Laucala lagoon, through the gap in the reef, and into the open sea.

He hoped to catch some large fish, but when he looked across the ocean he saw several black clouds mounting up from the horizon. The wind was turning and freshening, and he knew the signs. He gave up any thought of fishing and set his sail to tack back to land against the wind. But the offshore wind turned into a gale, and steadily and relentlessly the canoe was blown further out to sea.

Fortunately the island of Beqa was not far away, and he managed to steer his canoe so that the canoe reached this island. Exhausted by his struggles, he walked up the beach and came to a village where he was given a great welcome.

The most important chief of Beqa ordered his people to prepare food for the visitor.

"Just cook via," he said, and they took him at his word. A tremendous feast of via was prepared.

While he was waiting for the food to be cooked, the Rewa chief noticed one of the younger women, and was so attracted by her appearance and carriage that he resolved immediately to ask for her in marriage.

When his request was made known, a meeting of chiefs was held. The great yaqona bowl was brought out, and while the chiefs observed the ancient ceremonial, the visitor's request was discussed.

He waited apprehensively until the council's decision was brought to him.

"If you can eat all the food we have cooked for you, you may marry the young woman you desire and take her home with you to Rewa."

The young chief began to eat the meal. Fortunately he was hungry, and he enjoyed the new food. But after his second, third, and fourth large helping, the edge of his appetite was sadly blunted.

Yet he had fallen so deeply in love with this girl that he kept on eating. Every time he looked up he saw the faces of his hosts clustered round him, watching him seriously to see how he would meet his ordeal.

But the feast that had been prepared was more than any mortal man could digest, and the chief reached the end of his endurance. Getting to his feet as quickly as he could, he ran painfully out of the house towards his canoe. As he went, he noticed a bundle of the via plants lying outside one of the houses, and he snatched it up as he ran. He jumped into his canoe, hoisted his sail, and sped across the sea with a following wind.

His aspirations to marry the young woman were doomed to disappointment, but at least he brought a wonderful gift to his own people. When he reached his village he planted the via, which flourished; and ever since there has been an abundance of this staple plant over the flat lands of the delta of the Rewa river.

THE VINE THAT STOOPED OVER TONGA

THIS is a story of a magic vine that grew on the hills of Kadavu. News had come to this island of the beautiful daughter of the king of Tonga. The descriptions were so exciting that many young chiefs in Fiji sailed across the ocean to Tonga to see her.

One after the other they proposed marriage to her, but she refused them all.

When Naitokowalu, a young chief of Naibutobuto, the highest mountain in eastern Kadavu, heard of her, he made up his mind to go to see her too.

It was no ordinary voyage that Naitokowalu planned. He went straight to the goddesses who owned the magic vine, and asked them to transfer him to the distant land of Tonga by means of the vine. To this they agreed.

Naitokowalu immediately ordered his people to collect vast quantities of yams, dalo, kumala (sweet potatoes), vavudi (short cooking bananas), kawai (white vegetable something like potato), and pigs, and these were piled up into an enormous heap.

When the day came for him to leave, he went to the goddesses who caused the vine to put out a shoot which appeared at his feet and began to grow rapidly upwards. Naitokowalu's servants placed the food on the branches of the vine, and the goddesses explained to him the secrets he must know if he was to keep the vine under control. They told him that it would continue to grow until two red and yellow leaves appeared, instead of the green ones. When this happened, he would know that the vine had reached the limit of its growth, and would begin to bend and stoop down to the Tongan islands, 400 miles away. They also explained to him what would happen when he reached Tonga, and the signal that he should give for its return.

Naitokowalu sat on a stout tendril, and the vine shot upwards through the clouds and far out over the ocean, until at length the two red and yellow leaves appeared. As soon as this happened the vine stopped growing and began to bend at the top.

It seemed no time at all to Naitokowalu before the tip of the vine touched the shore of Tonga and began to creep along the beach and up the trees. He stepped down, and commanded the vine to unload the food which he had brought, after which he said, "Disappear!" As soon as the word was spoken the vine disappeared as though it had never been there.

The young chief walked to the nearest house and hid inside it. He had chosen one which was owned by an old woman. He had brought some food with him which the old lady cooked, and they had a meal together.

Now at that time there had been a drought in Tonga, and the people were nearly starving. When he heard this, the chief left the old lady's house with a basket of each kind of food that he had brought, and went to the king's palace. He did not go in at the main entrance, but by the back door, and told the servants that he had brought food for the royal family.

After this he went back again to the old woman's hut. It was an enormous surprise to the king and queen to receive food on their eating mat the next morning, but they did not question the unexpected fortune that had come to them. This went on for day after day, until a week had gone by.

The king told his servants that he would like to express his gratitude to the mysterious donor of the food, and that when the stranger came to the back door on the following day he was to be told that the king wished to see him.

When he heard the news, Naitokowalu dressed himself in the costume of his own country. He wore a large curved boar's tusk as a pendant, and from his waist to his knees he was covered in a skirt of many-coloured rushes. Over his shoulder he carried his war club, which was his insignia of rank.

The king received him graciously and thanked him for the gifts that he had brought, and asked him where he had come from. Naitokowalu replied, "I come from an island called Kadavu in the south of Fiji."

After the chief had been introduced to the queen, the young woman came in to see him. Because of her birth she was usually kept in seclusion, but as this was a special occasion she was allowed to unveil her face. As soon as the two young people looked into each other's eyes they knew that they were destined for each other.

The following day the princess told her father that she wanted to go to Fiji with Naitokowalu and become his wife. The same message was sent to the Fijian chief, and Naitokowalu sent a return message to say that they would leave in two days' time, and that he would then make the customary gift of whale's teeth and formally ask for her hand in marriage.

The next morning, still clad in his picturesque costume, Naitokowalu presented himself before the king, bearing three large whale's teeth. The king consented to the marriage, and accepted them as a token. Then he told the young Fijian that he would get his carpenters to build a large canoe in order that they might make the voyage.

Naitokowalu thanked the king for his offer, but told him that he would provide his own means of travel.

The next day came. At dawn the beach was crowded with people who had come from villages near and far, shedding many tears, and singing many songs of farewell.

But everyone was puzzled: was there no canoe to take the bridal couple to their island home?

"Now bid your daughter farewell," Naitokowalu said to the king and the queen. One after the other the nobles and their families came to take leave of their princess.

With his war club the Fijian chief smote the sand and muttered a few words. The astonished people saw the top of a great vine coming down to them from the clouds. It reached the edge of the beach, crept up along the sand, and up into the trees. The princess was placed comfortably in it, and the girl who was her chief attendant took her place by her side. Before Naitokowalu seated himself he gave the king the remainder of the stocks of food that he had brought with him. Then he took his place. Farewells were called, and Naitokowalu said, "O Vine, rise up!"

The vine rose up immediately, and its top was soon hidden in the clouds. When it reached Fiji it again bent over to Naibutobuto, the mountain home of Naitokowalu.

And what a homecoming it was! The young princess, who was now a married woman, admired the house that she was taken to, with its thick thatch and its ornaments of white cowry shells. The pillars were great vesi trees, with trunks eight feet in diameter, and the house itself was twenty-two yards long, ten yards high, and twelve yards wide.

Naitokowalu led his bride and her noble attendant into the home, and soon afterwards began the feasting and the ceremonies to celebrate the marriage of the Fijian chief and the Tongan princess. To this very day in the vicinity of that village a deep bathing pool commemorates in its name the coming of a Tongan lady to Naceva in Kadavu, for it is called Na nodrau sisili na marama Tonga: the bathing pool of the two Tongan princesses.

THE FIRST VADRA TREE

THE two sisters Ra Luve ni Toga and Ra Luve ni Kule were staying alone in the village. The older women had taken the great fishing nets of hand-made vau, with floats of light wood strung on a long rope of sinnet, down to the beach. The mother of the girls had given them final instructions before she left. She had been making masi or tapa, which was lying on the grass to dry in the sun. She said to her daughters, "Watch the tapa while I am away. If you see that rain is coming, take it into the house."

"Yes, mother," they said and, as young girls will, they promptly forgot what she had told them.

They went into the house, shut the door, and lay down to sleep. A shower of rain swept across the lagoon, over the beach, and across the grass, but they knew nothing of it. The beautiful tapa cloth became soaked, and was tossed about in the wind until it was torn and finally blown out to sea.

The bad weather had made fishing difficult for the women, but they caught some fish, and were returning home when the girls' mother noticed her torn tapa cloth floating on the water.

She went straight to her home and gave the girls a good talking to. They looked outside sleepily, and were surprised to find that the tapa had gone.

"You bad girl," the woman said to Ra Luve ni Toga. "Get out of my sight; I never want to see you again."

The girl was frightened because her mother was so angry. She ran outside, followed by her young sister, and they ran on until the village was some distance away. Then Ra Luve ni Toga turned round and said, "Go back home, Ra Luve ni Kule. You must stay to help mother. But I have been such a bad girl that I must go away."

So Ra Luve kept on running until she came to another village, where the people allowed her to stay. One of the young men fell in love with her and asked her to be his wife. She was feeling very miserable, and she agreed readily. She was nearly grown up, and she settled down quite contentedly as a wife. Unfortunately her husband's elder brother had also fallen in love with her, and wanted her so badly that he tried to kill her husband, so that he could take her for himself.

He made his plans cunningly.

"On the outer reef," he said to his brother, "there is a giant clam that would provide a wonderful meal for us. I want you to come to help me get it."

Ra Luve's husband suspected his brother's design, and he said to his wife, "Keep a close watch. If you see red on the water of the reef you will know that I am close to death. If it is black water that you see, you will know that I am dead."

Ra Luve ni Toga kept watch on the beach. The sea was rough as she watched the two men paddle in their canoe towards the reef. It had been the elder brother's intention to overturn the boat and kill his brother. As the young woman watched, the boat turned upside down, and she saw a shark attacking one of the two men.

Who could it be? Was it her husband, or was it his wicked brother? To her great relief she saw that it was the elder brother who was attacked and killed by the shark. Her husband turned the canoe the right way up, climbed on board, and was soon back on the beach with his wife.

"Let us always be happy together," they said. "Let us leave all our friends and stay by ourselves."

They said goodbye to the other villagers, and stood alone together on the beach. When their friends came to look for them, all they could see was a single vadra tree. As the two young lovers, the husband and wife, had clung together, they had been turned into a tree, the trunk of which was formed from the body of the man, while his wife provided the leaves and fruit. This was the first vadra tree that was ever seen in Fiji.

CHAPTER XV

FOLK TALES

THE BOY WHOSE NAME WAS ONE-HAIR

THE people of Udu, which is a little village on the island of Kabara in the Lau group, were greatly excited, for they had been invited to a wedding in the Tokelau group of islands.

They prepared a large supply of food, floor mats, tapa, whales' teeth, and yaqona to take with them. The only people who remained in the village were folk who were sick or very old, and one elderly, childless couple. This man and woman had both prayed to their gods to send them a child. One day, while the rest of the villagers were away, an old man came to the door of their house, and said, "I have come to give you a child."

He said nothing more, but went away. They wondered what was going to happen, and they did not have long to wait. The very next morning they saw a little boy standing near their kitchen, and they knew him to be the child who had been promised to them. They ran to him, and took him into the house, giving him food to eat.

He was a peculiar looking little boy, with a bald head except for one single hair on the very top of his head. With his shining scalp and his one black hair sticking up, he looked very funny; but they did not mind, because he belonged to them.

"What shall we call him?" they asked each other.

The husband smiled and said, "Let us call him One-Hair!" They looked at each other and nodded.

"Dear little One-Hair," they called. "Come here, One-Hair, and have something to eat."

Little One-Hair had a huge appetite. They were so pleased that he belonged to them that at first they did not mind. But after a while they became tired of providing him with such large meals, because One-Hair didn't grow at all. After four months of eating all the food they could possibly find for him, he still had not grown one inch.

Then their pride and love turned to disappointment, and even to hatred.

"Let's get rid of him," said the husband to his wife. "I have thought of a wonderful plan."

He made an earth oven. He called the little boy to him and said, "One-Hair, come here. Get into the oven with this food."

"Yes, Father," said One-Hair obediently.

The man covered him over and then went into the house.

"That's done!" he said to his wife. "He's in the oven. I've covered it all over, so we shan't be troubled with him any more – the greedy little wretch. I was sick to death of him!"

"Oh, good!" said his wicked wife.

After two hours had gone by, and it was time for the oven to be opened, the man went back to it to dig out the yams and fish so that he and his wife could have a good meal. As he drew near to the oven he heard a voice saying, "Father, Father, our food is cooked. Come and uncover it."

Feeling his own hair rising on his scalp, the man uncovered the oven, and out jumped the little boy.

"The oven was too hot," he said. "It made me perspire terribly."

Father and child went home together, and there was nothing to do but to give the boy another meal. One-Hair ate up all the yams and fish that had just been cooked.

After they had gone to bed at night, the foster father and mother of One-Hair talked together.

"We must find another plan," they said.

"I know," said the man. "Tomorrow will be a good day for fishing. I'll take him with me."

Next morning he picked up his fish trap made of kawa vine, or supplejack. It looked just like a big basket. One-Hair helped him to carry it down to the shore, and they waded into deep water with the trap, which had been weighted with stones.

"I am going ashore to make an oven ready for all the fish that we shall get," he told his adopted son. "I want you to stay here to look after the trap."

Then he seized the little boy, thrust him inside the basket, and lowered it into deep water. He hurried away, and the two elderly people congratulated themselves on having got rid of One-Hair at last.

That night it was cold, and they were sure that the boy would never survive.

In the morning the man hurried out to raise the trap. He was certain that it would be full of fish, and that the dead body of One-Hair would also be there. As he drew the trap up to the surface he heard a voice: "Father, Father, it has been such a cold night. I was so cold I might have died."

The two of them went home together. As soon as the woman saw the little boy coming she said, "Oh dear!" and began to cry.

"Here is the fish," the man said to his wife. "I suppose you'd better cook it."

She stopped crying and prepared a meal for the three of them. They sat down and ate together sadly, because One-Hair had at last realised what they were trying to do to him.

"You are tired of me," he said. "Twice now you have tried to kill me. But you don't do it the right way. I know how to do it. Listen to me, and do as I say, and then you will be rid of me for ever."

They listened carefully as he went on. "Cut off my one hair, and I shall die – it's as easy as that."

Neither of the old people said anything, but went on solemnly eating their fish and dalo.

After the meal, One-Hair lay down on the mats to sleep. As soon as his eyes were shut, the two villagers of Udu took a sharp shell and cut off the boy's single hair.

After that they went to sleep. In the morning One-Hair lay dead on the sleeping mat; and when the other villagers returned from the wedding in the Tokelaus, the couple were living alone without any child to comfort them.

THE WOMAN WHO EMPTIED THE SEA

THE little village of Lovoni lies in a valley far from the coast of Ovalau. It is so far inland that in the old days some of the inhabitants had never seen the ocean.

Amongst the stay-at-homes at Lovoni was an old woman who had lived all her life in the village. One day she wanted salt to put with the vegetables, but found that there was none left in the village. So she decided to do something that she had never done before – to travel to the sea to bring back salt water in which she could cook her vegetables.

She took a large gourd, tied it on her back with string made with coconut fibre, and set out on the long journey. The sun beat fiercely on her as she climbed up the narrow track that led up the mountains, but at length she reached the top, and for the first time looked out over the ocean. It stretched even to the world's end. About two miles out there was a coral reef. Below her she saw a shallow lagoon. The tide was in, and the reef was covered with water.

The old woman of inland Lovoni knew nothing about tides. When she saw the vast expanse of water she cried, "Oh! what a lot of salt water the chief of this village has!"

She hurried down the path to the seashore, dipped her gourd and filled it with salt water. Then she lifted it on to her back, arranging the plaited straps skilfully round her shoulders so that the water would not spill, and toiled up the hill again. When she reached the top she looked back. To her amazement saw that there was little water between the beach and the reef. While she had been walking the tide had gone out.

"Oh!" she said, "the chief will be angry because I have taken all his water! What a thief I am. I must give his water back to him before he misses it."

She turned round and went down to the shore, and poured the water back into the sea.

It was dusk by the time she reached the top of the ridge, but there was enough light for her to see that the water had again filled the space between the reef and the shore.

"Oh! How glad I am that I gave the chief back all his water!" she said. "He will not be angry now," and with her mind at rest she walked down hill to Lovoni with her empty gourd.

THE BOY WHO WAS HUNGRY

RAVAKA, the son of a chief of Rotuma, was only a little boy, but he had such a healthy appetite that it took four strong men to carry his food to him at meal times. The men would stagger into the house with their heavy loads of yams, dalo, coconuts, and fish, and Ravaka would eat everything that was put before him.

As he grew older and bigger, his appetite grew too, so that it now took many men to keep him supplied with food. The villagers became worried, and finally they went to the chief and explained that it was impossible for them to keep his son supplied with food.

The chief considered the matter and decided that as Ravaka's appetite could not be curbed, the only thing that he could do was to free the people of one district from all other work so that they could devote all their time to growing food for Ravaka.

Having selected a village he thought would be suitable, he sent his son there. Before long Ravaka returned to his father and said, "Father, the people of Nao'tau won't give me enough to eat!"

The chief then sent his son to Oinafa, but before many days were past, Ravaka returned and said, "Father, the people of Oinafa will not give me enough food to eat."

"Very well," said his father, "You must go to Fag'uta. That is a big village, and there will be plenty of food for you there."

Within a few hours Ravaka was back again, saying, "Father, the people of Fag'uta will not give me enough to eat."

This happened over and over again. Last of all the boy was sent to Malhaha. The villagers were ready to face the challenge. They planted larger gardens, caught wild pigs in the mountains and fed them on coconuts to make them large enough to satisfy Ravaka's appetite, while every day vast quantities of fish were caught, to keep him happy.

At last the hungry boy was supplied with sufficient food. The chief was so pleased that he gave more land to the people of Malhaha. Today, of all the districts in Rotuma, Malhaha is the largest. That is the reward that the villagers received for satisfying the hunger of that growing boy.

THE ETIQUETTE OF EATING

IF it were not for the kindness of the people of Wailevu, the villagers of Natumua would never have been able to eat fish. Natumua is a little village in the hills, far away from the sea, but like everyone else, the people of Natumua are fond of fish. They have a very happy way of making their requests known.

They go into their gardens and pick healthy, green leaves of dalo, and choose ripe brown coconuts from the trees. They remove the fibrous covering of the coconut by striking it on a pointed stick placed in the ground. Then the rich white flesh is grated on a sharp shell – or in these days on a jagged piece of iron fastened to the end of a slab of wood. The grated nut is squeezed into water, strained, and cooked with the dalo leaves.

When this appetising dish, which is called rourou, has been prepared, the women of Natumua go down to the village of Wailevu and present it to the fishermen and their wives.

As soon as this happens, the Wailevu people take their nets and wade out into the sea, where they are usually able to net many fine fish at once. They are experienced fishers and know where to go and how to catch the best fish, which they give to the waiting people of Natumua.

It is a happy arrangement; but in order to preserve the courtesies of the occasion, no Natumua person will ever eat rourou in the presence of anyone from Wailevu without asking permission.

In the same way, a Wailevu man will say to a Natumua man "May I eat this fish?"

These courtesies are observed wherever the people of Wailevu or Natumua may be, and the custom is observed to this very day.

A PETRIFIED FEAST

A CHIEF of Naqalotu invited some friends from the nearby village to come to a great feast. His people had been busy for several days preparing food. A huge oven had been dug and lined with stones, pieces of wood had been burnt to produce embers, the hole had been lined with leaves, and dalo, yam, breadfruit, turtles, fish, and fowls had been placed on the leaves, covered with soil, and another fire lit on top.

The oven had been left for hours. When it was opened with a digging-stick it was found that the food was cooked to perfection. Nuts had been grated, and coconut cream made ready to cook the prawns. Dalo had also been grated, mixed with sugar cane juice and grated coconut, and boiled in a banana leaf as a pudding.

All was in readiness for the guests who were travelling along the narrow tracks between the trees, when a man rushed into the clearing. He had come from the next village, Yakita.

"Fire! Fire!" he shouted.

Everyone joined in shouting, "Fire! Fire!" They all jumped up from where they were seated and ran along the track to Yakita.

If you visit Naqalotu today you will still see the remains of that feast in the form of stones. Some have the shape of turtles and others of fish, some are like dalo, and some like yams. They say that because the food for the feast had been neglected, it was turned into stone.

The land itself was bewitched that day, because nothing grows in Naqalotu but guavas and she-oaks, which are always found on barren ground.

THE FIRE WALKERS OF BEQA

In a house in Beqa some chiefs were sitting on the mat floor, as one after another related old legends of their people. The yaqona bowl passed from hand to hand, and the talk went on long into the night.

"What will you give me tomorrow for my story?" one of them asked. Each chief promised to bring him something.

Tui Qalita said, "I shall bring an eel."

The stories went on, but at the first light of morning the chiefs were sleepy and lay down to get some rest. When they woke, those who had promised to bring gifts went out to get them.

Tui Qalita went to dig for his eel, but it was difficult to find one. He dug and dug, throwing up mud and earth. A strange, semi-human creature emerged from the hole.

"Do not kill me," the creature said. "Save my life and I will be your God of War."

"No," Tui Qalita said. "I'm going to kill you."

"Please spare my life and I will reward you with useful goods, and many wives."

"No," Tui Qalita said again. "I have all the goods that I want, and more wives than I need."

"Please spare my life," the creature pleaded, "and I will give you power to walk on hot embers and not be burned."

Tui Qalita was pleased with this thought, and he accepted the gift. The descendants of Tui Qalita have ever since been able to walk on hot glowing embers with the soles of their feet unburnt, and this is something that still happens today on the island of Beqa.

CHAPTER XVI

TALES OF ROMANCE AND ADVENTURE

THE DART-THROWING COMPETITION

THE island of Ovalau is only three miles wide, but in a deep inland valley, tucked away amongst the high hills, there lived a strong and numerous tribe.

While the chief was away, working on his plantation, his son Ragoneliwa called the men of the village together and suggested that they should all go down to the southern end of the island to a place called Davetalevu, and challenge the men there to a contest. The young men were delighted at the idea; but while they were discussing it Rangoneliwa's father entered the house where the men were sitting cross-legged, with yaqona passing in coconut cups from one to the other.

There was so much cheerfulness and animated conversation that the chief wondered what was happening.

"What is going on?" he asked.

"We are going to Davetalevu to challenge the people there to a dart-throwing contest," said his son, wondering whether his father would let them make the expedition. The chief agreed and told them that he would go with them.

Babaleca, the chief, led the way, war club over his shoulder; behind him a long line of men followed in single file until they emerged from the jungle and came to the track which led along the coast.

When they reached the village of Masova, a woman who was sitting outside her house grating nuts to make coconut oil, greeted them and asked whether they could help her in her task.

Babaleca said, "Excuse us, please, we are in a hurry."

They reached Nasinu, and there they halted, while the chief urged them all to do their best and bring honour to their district by winning the contest. As he was speaking, he happened to look down at his hands and noticed that there was dirt under his nails, for he had had no time to attend to his toilet when he came in from the plantation.

He cleaned his nails with a splinter of wood. The dirt fell on the ground, and it is said that the little hill that can be seen at Nasinu has been made from the scrapings of Babaleca's finger nails.

Eventually the party reached the village of Davetalevu. They were seen, and a man ran to the chief of that village. A few moments later the news was shouted out so that everybody could hear.

"The hill people of Duvaga have come to us," cried the messenger. "Our visitors have come. Tomorrow we shall hold a dart-throwing contest. Prepare a feast for the visitors quickly. Women, go and carry firewood. Women, go fishing. Men, bring in dalo. Men, get yams from the storehouse. Boys, grate nuts. Men, dig a big oven for cooking."

The chief went out to meet the visitors. As the two chiefs met they clapped their hands politely, and spoke to each other respectfully. Arrangements were made for the entertainment of the visitors, and that evening small girls decked in wreaths of leaves and flowers, their bodies shining with coconut oil, sat on the handwoven mats in front of the visitors, while others beat lengths of bamboo with sticks as an accompaniment to the action songs.

Yaqona was mixed and drunk to the accompaniment of the traditional movements and speeches. As soon as a man's coconut shell was empty he would call out, "Maca" (dry) and send the empty coconut shell spinning along the mat to the man who was seated cross-legged by the tanoa, or wooden yaqona bowl.

The visitors slept well that night. The women rose early in the morning, lit the fires, and preparations were made for the morning meal. After it was eaten, everyone went to the rara, or village green, to take part in the contest or to watch what was happening.

There was one thing that the visitors did not know. The ghosts of the dead Davetalevu people were there, together with the living members of the tribe, and they helped in the dart throwing. Unseen, one of the ghosts stood at the end of the field, and every time a Duvaga dart was thrown, the ghost would get in the way and stop it. In spite of this the visitors put up a good performance.

One after another the players had their turn. When it came to the turn of Ragoneliwa, the chief's son, he swung his body to and fro and then threw his dart with all his might. It passed high over the heads of the ghosts, travelled across the sea for many miles and landed on the island of Bau, where it broke off a piece of land, forming the island near Kaba Point.

On the island of Bau there was a young woman, the daughter of a chief, sitting in her house. The dart broke through the thatched walls of the house and fell at her feet. Adi Wati, the young woman, sent for one of her servants and told him to tell the thrower of the dart to come and collect it. The messenger realised that it had come from a long distance. He embarked in a canoe and paddled across to Davetalevu to take the message. He went so swiftly that the applause for that miraculous cast of the dart had hardly died down.

Ragoneliwa responded at once to the messenger's invitation. Landing on the island of Bau, he went straight to Adi Wati's house, stepped over the door sill, and stood before her.

The young woman looked up at him. Ragoneliwa was tall and well proportioned, and held himself with dignity. His body shone with coconut oil, and his lavalava of many stripes of vau leaves, dyed with purple and yellow dyes, looked gay and beautiful even in the shadows of the house.

As the young man looked at the girl he realised that this was the woman he had been waiting for all his life, but his heart was heavy in him, for marriages in these islands are made, not because lovers look into each other's eyes and find their destiny, but by parents selecting brides and bridegrooms who are suited to each other. For long they looked at each other, and then parted without a word.

The dart-throwing contest had been won by the people of Duvaga; but Ragoneliwa's feet dragged as his comrades rejoiced on the homeward way. He was carrying a memory in his heart, but nothing more.

In later years he married the daughter of a chief of his own island. When their first daughter was born he named her Adi Wati; and to this very day Adi Wati is a name that is often found in the families of Duvaga in Ovalau. It reminds the people of the village of the prowess of one of their chiefs in throwing his dart from Ovalau to Bau. But it does far more than that. It keeps alive that wonderful moment when a young chief and the daughter of a chief looked at each other – knew that they were made for each other, and parted – for ever.

THE TURTLE OF THE SKY KING

DESPERATELY Lekabai stretched out his arms in the wild welter of water and his hands unexpectedly struck the comfort of solid rock. Painfully he pulled himself out of reach of the waves and collapsed on a narrow ledge. He had been fishing in his small canoe not far from his village in Samoa when a sudden storm had risen and swept him out to sea. His canoe had been waterlogged and smashed, and he was at his last gasp when he'd found safety on this rock.

When he recovered he began to climb. The rock towered far above him until it was lost in the clouds. He found nothing to eat, but slaked his thirst from small pools of rainwater. Day after day he climbed, until he came to the clouds and passed through them.

Now he looked up to the sky. There were no clouds there, but there was still no end to this barren towering mountain. There came a night when, faint from lack of food, he collapsed into unconsciousness.

When he woke he was lying on soft yielding vegetation. The sun was shining, birds were singing in the treetops, and a warm gentle wind stirred among the branches. It was a sight to delight any man, but Lekabai felt lonely.

He missed the slow crash of surf on his native shores, the familiar coconut trees, the voices of his friends. The fair land of the sky was no home for this ship-wrecked Samoan.

The Sky King heard the sound of weeping. It was so unusual that he came down to investigate. He bent over Lekabai.

"Why are you weeping?"

Lekabai looked up through his tears and recognised the nobility of the man who had spoken to him.

"I am weeping because this is a strange land, and I miss my own land of Samoa."

"Dry your tears," said the Sky King. "I will lend you my own turtle to take you back to your country. All you have to do is to climb on its back. There are only two things to remember: on peril of your life, do not open your eyes until the turtle climbs out on to the beach. Put your hands over your eyes and keep them there until you are able once more to look upon your wife and friends."

He pressed his hands over his eyes and took no notice of fish, wind, or birds.

"And what is the second thing?"

The Sky King smiled. "As you have seen, we have no coconut trees in this world. When the turtle returns, give it a coconut, and a mat woven from coconut leaves. We shall plant the coconut and learn to weave our own mats by copying the one you send us.

Lekabai climbed on to the turtle's back and hid his face in his hands as he had been bidden. For one horrifying moment he thought he was falling to his death. Then he felt the turtle's back under his legs. Together they plummetted down through the air like a stone, and sank far under the waves. The rough skins of sharks rasped against him, and their voices shouted to him to open his eyes, that he might see and avoid the perils of the deep sea.

The turtle rose to the surface, and there were dolphins plunging in and out of the waves and saying, "Look! Here is your island of Samoa. See, your friends are waiting for you!" But Lekabai would not look.

The wind howled round him and shouted, "Look out! I will blow you into the sea if you don't open your eyes!" Still he would not look.

Night came, and in the morning the birds flew round his head, screaming, "Is this the land you are looking for? There are palms and sandy beaches, and tall mountains; look and see if this is the island you seek."

But Lekabai remembered what the Sky King had told him. He pressed his hands over his eyes and took no notice of fish, wind, or birds. At last he heard waves breaking and felt the sand under his feet. As the turtle climbed out of the water he opened his eyes and saw the trees and the canoes of his people on the beach. Jumping off the turtle's back, he ran to his own village, where he was greeted as one who had returned from the Spirit Land. His wife and children were waiting for him, and all that day there were tears and laughter and the eating of good food, and rejoicing because Lekabai had come back to his people.

It was only when the sun was setting that Lekabai remembered the turtle, and the coconut, and the mat he had promised to send to the Sky King. With a feeling of dread clutching his heart, he rushed to the beach. There was no sign of the turtle.

During Lekabai's absence it had grown tired of waiting. It had swum out to the reef in search of seaweed to eat, and there it had been speared by fishermen coming back to land in their canoes.

The troubled men went to the far end of the beach where he

TALES OF ROMANCE AND ADVENTURE 245

could see a knot of men. They were heating an oven, and close by lay the dead body of the turtle they were preparing to cook.

"Iau-e! Iau-e!" he wept. "This is my good friend the turtle, that brought me from the Sky Land. What have you done? The Sky King will be raging, and much evil will come from the killing of his turtle."

His friends wept with him, until Lekabai said, "We have shed tears, but they will not help us. Put out the oven fires and let us bury the turtle. The Sky King must not know what we have done. If we bury it in a deep grave he will not know what has happened to it."

The terrified villagers dug such a grave as no man had ever seen before. Five days they spent digging it. As the hole went deeper and deeper, they lowered a tall coconut palm into it, so that they could climb up with the soil as it was excavated.

On the sixth day they lowered the turtle to the bottom and filled in the hole; and to make certain that the Sky King would temper his anger if ever he discovered what had happened, they placed a coconut and a woven mat beside the body of the turtle.

But the Sky King knew what had happened. He sent a sandpiper, which arrived as the grave was being filled in. It swooped down from the sky, touched a boy named Lavai-pani with its wing, and returned to its master.

Perhaps the Sky King was satisfied with the gifts that had been buried, for he did not punish Lekabai; but Lavai-pani, the boy who had been touched by the Sky King's bird, never grew to manhood. Year after year he remained a child. His friends became men and married and had children, who grew up and were married and had children. Through these long years Lavai-pani remained as a boy who would not grow up.

Lekabai was dead. Men sometimes talked of his adventures in the Sky Land and how he had returned to his home on the back of a turtle; how it had been killed and buried, but the place of its burial was now forgotten. Only Lavai-pani knew, and he did not talk to anyone.

The legend of the Sky King's turtle was told to the king of the Islands of Tonga. His eyes sparkled when he heard of the size of the turtle. He called his people to him and said, "You must go by sea to Samoa and find that turtle for me. Its shell will be well preserved. Dig it up and bring it to me, and from it I shall make fish hooks as large as the ones our grandfathers used."

So a large canoe sailed off to Samoa. When the crew landed and told the Samoans what their king had sent them for, they were laughed at.

"It is an idle tale," said the children of Lekabai's children's children. "It may well be that our ancestor went to the Sky Land and returned on the back of a giant turtle, but no man now living can tell you where it was buried."

The Tongans returned and reported to their king that the turtle's grave could not be found. He was angry with them. "Return at once," he said. "If you do not bring me the turtle shell I crave, I will have you killed."

They went back on what they feared was a fruitless quest. Seeking out the oldest men in the village, they besought them to search their memories and tell them where the grave might be found; but the greybeards talked amongst themselves and laughed, and could tell them nothing.

Then Lavai-pani, the boy who had been with them as long as they could remember, said, "Let not your souls be small, men of Tonga. I can tell you where the turtle is buried. I was there before these old men were born."

He took them to a place near the beach and said, "Dig here. This is where the turtle is."

All day the Tongans dug, while the Samoans stood and jeered. "Where is your turtle?" they asked mockingly. "The exercise is good for you, but you have simple souls if you trust this boy."

Then the Tongans turned on Lavai-pani with bitter words. "You have misled us. Tell us where the turtle is buried. If we do not find it we are dead men, and we will take you with us to the Spirit Land."

Lavai-pani, who had never before been heard to laugh, doubled up with mirth.

"See how foolish these Tongans are," he said to his people. "Twice they have sailed across the sea and now, after so little digging, they are ready to give up their quest."

He turned back to the visitors.

"Please yourselves," he said. "Go home to your king and tell him you have failed, if you wish. But I tell you that if you keep on digging for four days you will find the shell."

Remembering that their king would keep his word if they failed, they endured the taunts of the Samoans, and on the evening of the fifth day they found the shell and the bones of a gigantic turtle; but of the mat and the coconut there was no sign.

They sped back to Tonga; but on the way they talked together and decided that if they kept one piece of the shell for themselves it would never be missed. But the king was not deceived.

"There are only twelve pieces here," he said fiercely. "Where is the thirteenth piece?"

The men looked at each other and were tongue-tied. Then one, bolder than the others, replied, "O King, it is the fault of the people of Samoa. They said to us, 'Be satisfied with the twelve pieces. We will keep one for ourselves in order that we, too, may make fish hooks from it.'"

The king frowned.

"Are you afraid of the Samoans?" he asked. "My anger is more to be feared than theirs. Go back once more and bring that piece to me."

The king himself went down to the shore to see them leave. Their hearts were shrivelled in them, for they dared not go to Samoa again, nor return to their own village.

So they sailed on before the wind until they saw land. They were weary of the endless march of the waves, and put gladly to shore.

The place they came to was Kadavu, which was under the lordship of the King of Rewa. He took the Tongans to his own country and gave them land, and there they took wives and built houses, and lived with the people of Rewa. And that is how the people of Tonga first came to the islands of Fiji.

THE FLOOD THAT CARRIED A FEAST

ALONG the southern coast of Kadavu the canoes travelled backwards and forwards all day long between two villages. It was the occasion of a great feast, because the son of the chief of Joma was to be married to Nailevu, the beautiful daughter of the chief of Nabukelevu. Valuable presents were exchanged – whale's teeth, great bundles of mats made from woven pandanus leaf, sinnet, pottery, wooden pillows, food baskets, cloth made from beaten bark, coconut shells full of oil, fans, and immense quantities of food.

There had been ceremonial yaqona drinking, and vast mounds of turtles, fish, crabs, prawns, dalo, and yam had been eaten at the feasts.

When the three-day marriage ceremonial was over, Ratu Vuni and his young wife were left alone in their own home.

The weeks and months went quickly by. In due time it was announced that Nailevu was to become a mother. According to Fijian custom, husband and wife must be separated at this time. Nailevu was taken back to her own home. When a son was born there was great rejoicing and a runner was sent quickly to convey the news to Ratu Vuni. The chief knew that he must send some substantial gift to his wife's people, but this was a real problem to him, for at this time there were no canoes at his village.

The chief went to the hill village of Niudua, a mile or two up the river, and presented a basket of coconuts to the priest.

"I want your help," he said, and told the priest about his problem.

"Sir, all will be well. Return to Joma. I shall see that the ceremonial gift of food will follow you, and that it will be taken at once to Nabukelevu."

Ratu Vuni wondered how the priest was going to do this; but before he had reached his home, torrents of rain began to fall. The sky was lit by lightning, and thunder roared amongst the hills. The rain continued unceasingly, floods of water dashed down the hillside, and swollen streams overflowed their banks. All night long the rain continued, and again on a second day and a second night. When Ratu Vuni awoke on the third day the rain was still falling and the mountain streams had become raging torrents. Dalo plants by the thousand were being swept out of the gardens on the river banks.

This was the gift that the priest was arranging for his chief to send to Nabukelevu. But he made a mistake. It occurred to him that dawa timber would also be acceptable; and as soon as the thought came into his mind, great dawa trees were swept along in the flood. Some of the villagers realised that he had made a mistake, and called to him hurriedly, "Our chief does not want timber included in the gift!" By the power of thought the priest directed the dawa timber to the bank, where it stranded.

In the meantime the flood swept the dalo roots into the main stream and past the home of the chief of Joma. The rain stopped and the sun came out.

"Good!" exclaimed the chief. The stream of dalo roots went out between the mango forests to the sea, was carried westwards along the Kadavu coast, where the current turned sharply at right angles and went through the calm waters of the lagoon of Nabukelevu.

Nailevu's father was standing on the shore. He was astonished at the sight that met his eyes; but when he realised that this novel method of sending dalo originated with his son-in-law Ratu Vuni, he was pleased, and graciously accepted the gift.

THREE PRESENTS
FOR THE CHIEF'S DAUGHTER

VATULELE is a beautiful island where coconut palms fringe the white sandy beaches, and the south-east trade winds softly blow. The island lies a little distance from the coast of Nadroga.

At one time a beautiful young woman of high birth lived in this lovely place, admired and loved by all her people. But on the mainland there were daughters of other chiefs who resented the praise that was given to her. The more the young woman of Vatulele was praised, the more jealous they became.

She had many suitors, among them the chief of Lomaiviti. He wondered what was the most suitable present he could give to her, and after much thought decided that the best gift would be a beautifully carved polished war club which belonged to his tribe. It had killed many men and was greatly revered, and there was nothing he could think of that would be a more suitable gift when he asked the young woman of Vatulele to marry him.

He had to obtain the consent of the elders of the tribe. When they knew that he wanted it to try to gain the favour of the Vatulele woman, they agreed.

So his men prepared a canoe, loaded it with baskets of food, and went aboard. The canoe skirted the coast of Viti Levu, travelling past Naselai, Nukulau, and Suva Bay, where the small village of Suva nestled among the palms and the ivi trees, past Navua and Serua, until it came to Vatulele, the coral island on the reef off the coast.

The chief and his men were courteously received. Speeches were made, food was eaten, and a great deal of yaqona was drunk. But when it came to the real purpose of the visit, the young woman refused to marry the chief. Greatly crestfallen, he was forced to return to his home at Lomaiviti.

The next suitor was a chief of Ba, which lies at a little distance up the coast of Nadroga. His journey took him out of the mouth of the Ba river, past Lautoka, Nadi, Lomawai, and Cuvu, past the mouth of the Sigatoka river, and to the beach at Vatulele.

His present was a beautiful skirt, coloured purple and yellow and red and black. Many vau leaves had gone into the making of it. The dyes had been prepared from shellfish and mud and the bark of trees, and the waistband was finely woven.

The young woman took one look at the skirt and said, "No, thank you. I don't want the skirt and I don't want you."

The next young man who aspired to wed the girl was a chief of Nadroga. The best present that he could find was a large, smooth stone which lay on the beach. He put it into his canoe, and when he reached Vatulele he told the young chieftainess that this stone was for her to sit on outside her house, whenever she felt like doing so.

The girl was thrilled. She sat on the stone and looked at the young man, her eyes shining with joy.

"Will you marry me?" he asked.

"Yes, I would like to marry you," she said.

And so, with all the pomp and ceremony of a chiefly Fijian wedding, the beautiful young woman of Vatulele and the chief of Nadroga were married.

They had many children, and today the descendants of the two families are closely united in affection and loyalty. Those who look may still see the stone that the young man gave to his bride, standing near the shore at Vatulele. But what this story really proves is that love is more important than gifts!

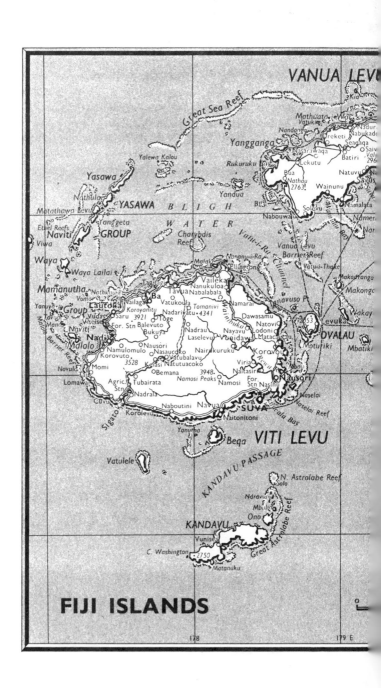